DREAM DIE REPEAT

Jules Langton x

JULES LANGTON

Published by Goldcrest Books International Ltd
www.goldcrestbooks.com
publish@goldcrestbooks.com

ISBN: 978-1-913719-44-9
eISBN: 978-1-913719-45-6

For Tom, Emily, James and Luca ... my world.

EARLY REVIEWS

I absolutely loved the book, never quite knew what was coming next. I found the descriptive writing draws you in to feeling that you are almost watching it while you are reading.

It was exciting but also intriguing and at times I was on the edge of my seat with the suspense.

I liked the main character, Ellie, and even though she seemed to have it all going for her, with a lavish lifestyle and money being no object, I felt sorry for her and was happy that she seemingly found happiness as the story unfolded. I was certainly not ready for the twist near the end of the book but this has left me eagerly awaiting book 2

I was hooked from page one and highly recommend it 10/10

Jules's debut novel, Dream, Die, Repeat, is a real page-turner. From the very first paragraph, the reader is given a glimpse of the unknown that leaves us wondering. We are then taken on a journey from the high-life in London to the ruggedness of Yorkshire through the main character, Ellie, and her transformation. Jules's obvious knowledge of Whitby and the surrounding area comes through on these pages that allows the reader to truly visualize where the story is taking place. The inclusion of music and song titles that are interspersed throughout the book add to the overall mood. By the end of the book you are left with only one question… when does book number two come out?

PROLOGUE

On that bright autumn morning, I could see the forest just beyond the river, the trees displaying their brilliant colours; red, copper, and yellow leaves glistening like jewels in the sunshine. Hands and feet bound, no point in struggling, this was my fate. My long dark hair, matted and untamed, masked my face and my fear.

I wore no clothes, my naked body shivering with scant warmth offered from the sharp autumn sun. On my pale, coldly mottled skin, the only blemish was the heart-shaped mole just above my right breast. I was mute, no strength left to curse those around me, and I chose not to satisfy them with my terror. Closing my eyes, I said a silent prayer and waited for the inevitable. From the hushed silence around me, I knew it was time.

The shock of the cold hit me as I was lowered into the river. It wasn't long before I was fully submerged. I knew I was going to drown. Was it to be lingering, or would merciful unconsciousness come quickly once my lungs filled with water? I began to sink deeper into the icy cold, swallowed water, tried not to breathe in through my nose. Confusion, jumbled tumbling thoughts, I was light-headed and there was a sharp pain in my chest as the water finally and inevitably robbed me of my last weak breath…

Waking with a jolt, I took a few gasping breaths, heart beating like a drum, dull ache in my chest, throat like sandpaper, and a minute or so to realise it was just another nightmare. This terrifyingly lucid dream had been plaguing me forever. Since childhood I've had a phobia of water, and visions of struggling and drowning have haunted my nights all through the years. In this particular dream the fear was so real, the scene so vivid. Sitting up amongst sweaty, tangled sheets, taking long deep breaths to calm the panic, I tried to shake off the horror.

CHAPTER 1

February

The insistent shrill of the alarm shocked me awake at 5.30 am and it didn't help that my head was banging after a particularly messy night out. Hauled out of another bad dream, I needed a minute or so to shake off the panic that always clung on for a good few minutes after I woke. The clock showed it was 1st February and I wasn't sorry to see January was over, the most depressing month of the year.

Still disorientated, I realised Charlie was asleep beside me and my heart sank. His over-6ft frame, naked apart from Calvin Klein boxers, was sprawled across my bed, taking up far too much room and creasing my hugely expensive Egyptian cotton duvet cover, which instantly put me in a bad mood. He was gym-toned because despite being a heavy social drinker he compensated with a diet and training obsession which included lots of protein shakes and weight training.

Yesterday evening we'd met up with friends, a noisy gathering straight from work, not rolling back to my apartment until well after midnight and much the worse for wear. His Champagne Charlie nickname had been earned because drinks were always more than free flowing when he was flashing the cash, treating everyone. 'One last one, Ellie,' he'd said towards the end of the night. Totally ignoring my 'Charlie, I have to be up for 5.30!' he made his way to the bar, returning with a round of Black Velvets, a combination of Guinness and champagne, the in drink of the moment. A small cheer went up from the surrounding crowd. I wasn't sure if they all qualified as friends, although they were happy to take advantage of his generosity. I didn't want to snap at him in front of everyone, but lately he'd been calling the shots in our relationship rather too readily, and I knew I'd regret it in the morning.

Charlie didn't need to wake until 7.00 and he didn't stir as I left the bed. Like me he was in advertising, working at one of our City of London competitors. As young professionals we lived a manic, high octane lifestyle, working and partying equally hard, offsetting time pressures and stress with the convenience of heading out straight from work, descending on a local wine bar, a favoured restaurant or sometimes to one of the managing partners' over-opulent penthouse apartments for insanely wild hedonistic house parties.

Charlie had been on the scene on a casual basis for the past seven months. I liked his easy, cheeky charm, his chat up line, "Nice to meet you, I'm Charlie, and you must be... gorgeous!" was knowingly cheesy, and made me laugh. He was also exceedingly easy on the eye, olive skin and striking denim-blue eyes. Conversation flowed, along with the drinks, and I learnt he'd lost his dad, who'd come to the UK from Italy, when he was a teenager. That explained his Mediterranean looks. I too had skin that tanned evenly and easily, even in the winter I had a nice glow. "Not sure where mine comes from," I gestured at my own face, "must be a throwback because both parents are natural blonds – could be Abba extras. I look nothing like them."

We hit it off, making each other laugh, and falling into an easy relationship, probably drinking too much but enjoying time together. Now though I kinda wanted my own space back. I knew it'd not been a good idea him staying over last night. Maybe things had run their course, I was easily bored with the men I found attractive, usual limit six months max. Charlie was probably past his sell-by date. It wasn't something I'd cry about, not something I was particularly proud of either, just all part of the circles in which we mixed and moved. My relationships – if they could be called that – were with other advertising types, traders, or lawyers, men I tended to meet at after-work minglings and there was no doubt they shared a certain arrogance and confidence, not to mention classic, chiselled good looks. I suppose they fell in line with my obsessive designer fashion purchases; as I said, boredom always set in swiftly.

I wasn't going to let the hangover from hell or Charlie's presence put me off my morning routine. I quietly put on my silk robe and slippers, and in the kitchen popped a couple of Paracetamol. Then I loaded bananas, kiwis, kale and nuts into the Nutribullet – always a fan of the latest fad – hoping a healthy breakfast shake would undo some of last night's damage; it also wouldn't harm my perfect size 6 figure, think Victoria Beckham, the look I aspired to.

The underfloor heating kicked in at 5.00 so the apartment had already warmed up nicely, the music system had automatically chosen a motivating playlist which came on as I walked into the bathroom, and under an invigorating cold shower, I started to feel half human again. I moisturised, added just a smudge of mascara and lipstick, and headed to the walk-in wardrobe. That had been the biggest selling point of this apartment, a whole room for my outfits – Carrie of *Sex and the City* would've killed for a wardrobe like mine. My designer outfits were, naturally, carefully colour co-ordinated with sections for bags, belts and shoes. I was heading for my morning gym session, and in coordinating gear, trainers, and hair neatly ponytailed made a quiet exit, as the last thing I wanted was a heavy conversation with Charlie.

A short but brisk walk along Richmond's high street with its boutiques, wine bars, and café pavement tables cheered me up a little. I'd lucked out when Rightmove presented me, just over two years ago, with an executive apartment in one of the most desirable areas of London, it even had a balcony overlooking the Thames. Over the past few years, I'd earned a six-figure salary supplemented with sizeable quarterly bonuses, so not only had I immediately snapped up the apartment but had been able to do it mortgage-free. Decorated throughout in muted grey and white, it had the industrial look I loved, wall-to-wall deep-pile charcoal carpets, and sheepskin rugs in all the right places, and fully furnished by an upmarket interior designer, ready to move straight in. There was a weekly cleaning and ironing contract set up with a local agency, which it would have been rude not to continue, especially as they quickly adapted to my strict regime of colour coding, and learnt I detested mess or clutter, so the place was always ultra-tidy, with the minimalist feel I relished.

When I moved in I'd taken gym membership, registered with the resident personal trainer and always got a workout done and dusted before my working day began. Sam the PT put me through my daily paces, resistance training, cardio, and spin, and had taken me at my word when I said I wanted him to be tough. "You look rough this morning," he greeted me, "heavy night? Well, don't think I'm going to let you off lightly." I groaned quietly; I knew he wasn't kidding. He didn't seem too cheerful himself as he continued to lecture me. "No point eating healthy, and sweating here, if you stay up all night drinking, Ellie." I gave him a sad puppy face, and muttered, "heavy day at work." But he wasn't wrong and I had recently been giving thought to my overenthusiastic alcoholic intake. Trouble was, good intentions went out of the window when I was out, non-drinkers were seen as antisocial in my network.

I got back to my apartment just over an hour and a half later feeling a little more energised. Charlie was up, rummaging around in the kitchen. "Hey, hon, make you one of my special shakes? I'm making one for me." He was doing a good job of invading my space and I'd recently had the uncomfortable inkling he wanted to take this relationship further. "I've told you before I'll sort out my own," I snapped, then softened it with, "Just concentrate on getting yourself up, and out!" as I headed into the bedroom. My earlier mood wasn't improving, despite all my gym exertions, and for some reason I still felt shadowed by that wretched nightmare, although I should be used to it by now, my night time hauntings always seemed intensified when I was particularly tired or stressed. But so much was riding on current workloads, slowing down wasn't an option, so I guessed I'd just have to put up with that black cloud hanging over my head.

My walk-in wardrobe never failed to perk me up. Outfits were always planned at the weekend for the working week ahead, so I knew exactly what I'd wear every day this week. Today it was a Stella McCartney, black pinstriped trouser suit, crisp white blouse with oversized collar, teamed with black patent Louboutin high heels, with their trademark red soles. Power dressing made me look and feel fabulous! Warmer shower this time and I washed my long hair, deep conditioned, moisturised again and followed with the makeup application which I had down to a fine art, then a spray of Chanel No 19 and I was ready to face the day. Without pausing I called Mike; having my own driver was one of the benefits of the job. He drove me to my city office and picked me up again at the end of the working day, taking me wherever I wanted which was, more often than not, straight out for drinks.

Comfortable in the back seat of the Mercedes, I still didn't feel relaxed and couldn't deny an anxious knot in my stomach at the thought of the workload ahead, which added to my throbbing head and dark mood, meant today wasn't shaping up well. Extracting my phone I did the swift, obligatory social media scan, aware I was far more obsessed with being liked than I should have been, and there was no doubting the disproportionate guilty pleasure I gained from receiving far more than most of my large numbers of friends and colleagues.

Like so many women in my 30-plus age-group, I liked to think I gave the impression of being super confident and ambitious. If that led people to think I had too high an opinion of myself, I didn't mind; so maybe there was a touch of arrogance there too, and if, as one ex-friend had once commented, selfish and shallow came into the mix, well so what? I wasn't that bothered – it was probably just jealousy talking. Posting pictures of my olive-skinned, nearly six-foot willowy frame, I knew I looked good – fact, not vanity – with high-end, immaculate designer clothes, and usually a guy or two on my arm. God forbid I'd ever allow myself to be tagged in a picture looking the worse for wear. But obviously keeping up my immaculate image came at a price. My hair was naturally dark brown, but most of the time I liked it blonde, for that sun-kissed look, and eyelash extensions and manicures were of course a necessity. Everyone knew not to take pictures of me unless I looked my ultimate best and naturally, I always looked happy, dazzling white smile, bee-stung lips, no lines, or crow's feet in sight. I was absolutely not reliant on Botox, fillers, or any of the other in-vogue treatments, but on the other hand it would be foolish not to take advantage now and then of what was out there. My work friends called me Beautiful Ellie, it was tongue-in-cheek, and I always laughed, but truth be told, I did feel all my efforts paid off rather well, although there were the occasional nagging doubts when it came to time spent online. Maybe it was because I was getting older, but it always made me smile when I saw younger work friends post on social media, during or after we'd been for lunch, coffee, or a night out. They'd spent the whole time glued to their screens, posting pictures and messaging without actually communicating with the people in front of them! It felt like Instagram versus reality and had been irritating me lately, which just fed into my feeling of things being out of balance, just not quite right.

Certainly that morning I felt flat and demotivated. Maybe I was sickening for something, or maybe it was starting to slowly dawn on me that whilst living exactly the life I'd always wanted, I wasn't really enjoying it that much anymore. Like a recurring, nagging toothache was the big question, now I'd reached the top; what next?

Mike pulled up near my office. "Here you go, Ellie!"

"Thanks, Mike, sorry, been a bit antisocial today! I'll give you a call when I finish later. Have a great day." I headed to the coffee shop a few doors down from the office for an extra-large, extra-hot, triple-shot latte, smiling ruefully as I walked away with it, acknowledging the only thing to give me real pleasure this morning was the promise of a super caffeine hit later. Taking the initial satisfying sips, I hurried through reception, and into the lift just as the doors started to close. On the tenth floor was Jones, Harper and Smith Advertising, where I'd worked since leaving university with a first class degree in advertising. Creativity, having always been my strength, together with a strong analytical mind, and a photographic memory, made me stand out amongst my peers.

I had little in common with my parents but I bless them for my work ethic and drive. Running their own long-established law practice they'd expected me to join the firm, but I'd disappointed them with a lack of any interest in law. I grew up – an only child – materially rich but emotionally poor, and busy parents had little time to spend with me so I was passed from one nanny to another, and then on to boarding school. I sometimes wondered why they had me at all. My upbringing almost certainly impacted on my emotional development, probably why I'd never committed to a long-term relationship, or perhaps it was simply that I had a low boredom threshold. There had never been any doubt in my mind that as a woman in the City I'd have to work above and beyond just to prove myself, and relationships did tend to get in the way of career success. Fair to say I'd put, if not blood, then plenty of sweat and tears into getting to where I was now and it was achieving this lifestyle that had motivated me, kept me buzzing. Was it now beginning to lose its shine? I'd celebrated my 30th birthday in October last year, and it wasn't a milestone I'd looked forward to, had in fact rather dreaded the day, and then I found that looking ahead to my thirties and forties was, quite frankly depressing.

Like everyone I had low days, but usually bounced back swiftly, however following my birthday I simply couldn't shake the underlying grumble of dissatisfaction and disconnection. I was most at ease and more myself with my university group than with all my more recent friends. Alice, Sarah, and Lizzie kept me grounded. They knew the real me, and had done since well before the high life I now led, and with them I never felt compelled to fulfil any expectations, and that uncomfortable trapped feeling fell away. It seemed crazy, I now had all the ingredients to make me truly happy, and I wasn't! Alice, Sarah, Lizzie and I had always confided in each other and I knew their input was always honest and sensible. The time had come to talk.

CHAPTER 2

Steaming coffee in one hand, cheeky cigarette in the other, I stepped out onto my balcony overlooking the Thames where spring sun sparkled on the water. I relished the luxury of a day off, and time to enjoy the view I loved, and for which I'd worked so hard. I was normally out of the house far earlier so never had the opportunity to see what went on below my apartment and was now fascinated by the hive of activity. Yummy Mummies jogging along the path, hanging on to designer pushchairs. Cyclists in full Lycra expertly if aggressively weaving in, out, and around pedestrians and tourists, and students out in force in rowing boats, kayaks, and on paddleboards. Stretching my impressively well-toned arms above my head after a particularly calm and blessedly dreamless sleep, I reflected that life was starting to feel a little less cluttered. I was definitely in a better state of mind.

I'd finished with Charlie a few weeks back, a tougher conversation than anticipated. He was genuinely disbelieving.

"I know you've been irritable and edgy, thought it was your workload though, not me." He paused for me to say something. I didn't. "Look," he said, "I want us to work, I think we're good together, give me another chance." He was sitting at the breakfast bar, and for a moment put his head in his hands. I hoped to goodness he wasn't going to cry, I really didn't do emotion, and am sorry to say I fell back on that old standard. "Honestly, Charlie, it's not you, you're a fantastic guy, it's me, just not in the right place for a relationship at the moment."

I'd also slowed down a whole lot on my party lifestyle and spent more time chilling at home, enjoying my own company. It was great to be able to catch up on *Suits, Sex and the City,* chill to music or impulsively opt for a long bubble bath with the works – candles, face-pack and a glass of chardonnay. Maybe I was turning into a hermit, but I was feeling far happier. I knew I had to make more drastic changes; but this was a start.

Today was for looking forward, not back. Alice, Lizzie and Sarah were coming to stay for the weekend, and we were planning Alice's hen party. She'd found her prince in Robbie, a charming Scotsman, and together they'd already established their own law firm, were growing themselves a rather formidable reputation, and were now sealing the deal by tying the knot. Alice was the first of our tight-knit group to get spliced, the wedding was in Edinburgh, and we were all bridesmaids, with the proviso that we had the final say on our dresses!

I had a couple of hours to kill before they all arrived and, relaxed as I was, fancied some mindless TV. I landed on *Coast*, a travel programme presented by long-haired Neil Oliver. He was exploring the seaside town of Whitby and the Yorkshire Moors. When I holidayed, it was almost always abroad, so I'd spent shamefully little time exploring my own British Isles. The scenery onscreen was absolutely beautiful and only enhanced by the Scottish lilt of the narration. I'd never been to the North East and the history of Whitby, with its twice-yearly Goth Festival, magical history, and Bram Stoker connection was fascinating, and couldn't have been timelier. I knew Alice, carbon footprint in mind, wanted to stay in the UK, and it seemed the next Goth Weekend would be at the end of April, exactly when we planned to hold the hen do.

I recalled a group I'd seen some months earlier. I rarely took the Tube but unusually Mike wasn't available to pick me up; first time that had happened during the working week and even odder, my father happened to mention he thought he'd seen Mike driving through their village around that time. I assumed he must have been booked by the firm to take someone else, or maybe he was doing a bit of moonlighting. Whatever the reason, I was not thrilled to join the masses heading underground, with the platform and trains full of people determined not to speak or even look at each other – headphones on, scrolling through phones or simply adopting a vacant expression and studiously avoiding eye contact with fellow travellers, in the way only Brits can.

On that particular afternoon though, there was a lively group of men and women in my carriage, and you couldn't help but stare. Head to toe in black, strangely and beautifully glamorous, they looked as if they'd come straight off a Gothic fashion shoot, faces extraordinarily pale, maybe makeup, maybe just in contrast to their clothing. Shamelessly listening in, I gathered they were in fact all young professionals, and quite high-powered at that. In their spare time they chose to be Goths. The odd thing was, at one point they'd all been discussing Whitby and the festival although it hadn't really meant anything to me at the time. But as Neil wound up the programme I remembered them, how incredible I'd thought they were and their conversation. I love a coincidence and how amazing would it be to have Goth as our hen party theme, and where else but Whitby for a setting that ticked all the boxes. I bet we could get costumes suited that would give the average Goth a run for their money, especially as Sarah was a fashion designer.

Lizzie was the first to arrive that afternoon. An Amazon of a woman, who'd inherited both height and beauty from her Nordic mother, long blonde hair, deep ice blue eyes and a pale, flawless complexion. She wore minimal makeup because she didn't need it, whatever she wore looked amazing on her tall thin frame and she had a metabolism that let her eat like a horse without putting on weight. Unsurprisingly she was a supermodel, now at the pinnacle of her career jet-setting around the world. Like me she'd planned a City career, but instead she was spotted by a talent scout fresh out of university, which totally changed her plans. A rather magnificent penthouse in Manchester, near to her parents, was her UK base.

Naturally she was unmatched in her ability to pack a capsule wardrobe and she dropped her miniscule case in the hall before giving me a long and enveloping hug from which we both emerged breathless but beaming. Still holding me by the arms she looked me up and down critically – I knew she'd say exactly what she thought, and thankfully it was, "You're looking amazing, love the dress." "Not looking too shabby yourself, darling," I grinned and we flopped, arm in arm on the sofa, to listen to the soundtrack I'd chosen from our university days. I'd selected 'Eple', by Röyksopp, specially for Lizzie. When I was on my own, I went for rather more moody, I knew when I closed my door, my music tastes didn't reflect how I presented myself to the world. But for a girls' gathering I made sure there were all our favourite tracks from all eras, and strictly upbeat.

Alice was the next to arrive, as small as Lizzie was tall, with luscious auburn hair (God save anyone who called it ginger) and the freckled complexion and emerald eyes which went with it, our beautiful Irish girl. People always underestimated Alice; her tiny frame, cute freckles on an upturned nose and soft voice, belied who she was. Time and time again we'd stood back and watched in amusement as she wiped the floor with some poor soul who'd crossed a line at uni or in a club or a pub. She was now a hugely sought-after, kickass lawyer, with a growing reputation for success – opponents taking her for a Chihuahua and only too late realising they were dealing with a Rottweiler.

Sarah was the last to arrive, not unusual, she was late for everything and in the past her tardiness had cost her grades at university, many dates, and indeed several great job opportunities. She was based in the Cotswolds, and ran a highly successful organic fashion house and although her time-keeping had never improved, these days she delegated a great deal to her team who were far more able to watch the clock. Living in her very own time zone – we called it Sarah Time – was still a pain for her friends, although we'd learnt over the years to always build in an extra hour, so when everyone else was told 3.00, Sarah was told 2.00 – which went some way to alleviating the problem. Despite this she arrived like a whirlwind, and breathless and dishevelled almost fell into my arms as I opened the front door.

At university Sarah had experimented with turning her hair all the colours of the rainbow, deciding what best suited her naturally light brown skin, and dark chocolate brown eyes, a nod to her mother's Indian heritage. Nowadays she stuck to a dark truffle shade for her short hair which set off her complexion and minimal makeup and was perfect for her gamin looks. Sarah knew however ruffled she was when she arrived, we'd always sort her out, although I always felt with her simple chic style and own organic designs, she looked gorgeous – ruffled or not! "Sorry, girls, I'm not that late, am I? Hugs?" Lizzie obliged and Alice, for whom being on time was almost a religion, forgave her with a quick peck on the cheek. Sarah's lateness was legendary but it was more than made up for once she arrived, when she had time to listen, hear and offer sage advice and practical help for all of us. Now, she flopped down onto the overstuffed sofa next to Lizzie and held out a grateful hand for the large glass of wine I'd poured. We'd all fallen in love with Sia, so I put on one of our favourite tracks, 'Titanium', in the background and, together again, we sat back and relaxed; bliss!

CHAPTER 3

April

I'd fretted for an age about what to pack for Alice's hen party – usually I was certain what to wear when, but the country casual idea took me right out of my comfort zone and having little experience of holidaying around the British coast, I didn't want to take any chances with the good old British weather. A major online spending spree later, I thought I'd finally got it right and had to say casual felt comfortable, and it was a relief not to be suited and booted as I was daily for work.

I knew I'd bought and packed far too much; choice of outdoor jackets, oversized khaki parka, and a Barbour jacket for a start, then my Hunter wellies, dressier black knee-high boots, and a variety of scarves, hats, gloves, cashmere jumpers, jeans and leather trousers. A capsule wardrobe it wasn't! And struggling down to the underground car park with my two large suitcases I briefly toyed with the idea of going back to the apartment and taking some items out but I'd already double-checked everything, turned off lights and locked up securely, so decided going back might be more stressful than going on.

Whilst I had Mike to drive me for day-to-day journeys, I'd kept my own convertible BMW, and setting the satnav for the five-hour drive to North Yorkshire, the heated massage seat on and the awesome Corinne Bailey Rae and equally amazing Celeste (her version of 'La Vie En Rose' was sublime) for listening pleasure, I thought it was one of the wiser decisions I'd made. I was looking forward to the drive and to time out of the office.

Each of Alice's bridesmaids had been given a different role in organising the hen party. I was in charge of accommodation. Leaving it quite late due to our busy schedules – we'd all had to confirm the time off work – I'd been worried I wouldn't find a hotel to meet our exacting standards but finally found what I was looking for, a 5-star hotel on a country estate convenient for Whitby. Nestled in acres of its own private grounds with a lake, country club, spa, gym, valet, and concierge service, it ticked all the boxes. Despite that, I still checked the reviews, as you can't be too careful. They were universally gushing so I went ahead.

Alice had insisted we have individual rooms at the hotel. Even though she happily shared when we pitched up to each other's places, she did prefer her own personal space. I'd expected to have little or no choice on our accommodation, so was delighted there were three queen-size rooms and one king available. Obviously, I reserved the king for Alice the bride-to-be, and the other three as well. I browsed the spa menu while I waited for the reservations office to confirm, and smiled at the thought of a deep tissue massage – my back had been tight and achy for what seemed like ages now, probably all that computer time. In fact, I thought I wouldn't just leave it to chance and went on to make some pre-bookings for treatments we'd all enjoy.

Lizzie was in charge of events, organisation having always been her forte. She did her research on the biannual Goth Festival and sent pictures of previous events. Festivalgoers certainly went to town when it came to outfits, Gothic glamour abounding but with lots of humorous touches. Apparently there were different genres which came under the Goth heading; Steampunks, Cybergoths, and those opting for Romanticism and Victoriana. Smiling at her efficiency as I read, I liked the idea of Romanticism and Victoriana, but wasn't so sure of the others, anything with Punk in it was not for me. Confirming she'd booked tickets, 'no backing out now,' Lizzie was particularly fascinated by Whitby's Bram Stoker and Dracula connections.

Our purchased tickets included the music festival, which Lizzie had ascertained was Gothic Rock and Synth-pop – "It may not be our normal thing," she said, "But we have to embrace the whole experience, look on it as our trip to the dark side!" She'd also booked us a private Ghost Walk on Saturday evening with Dr Will Sutcliffe, apparently an expert on the paranormal activity of Whitby. Spooky was obviously the order of the day. In her inimitable fashion and in double-quick time Lizzie had also created an itinerary, a copy of which we all received. We'd be exploring the coast, Moorland, Robin Hood's Bay, Staithes, and Runswick Bay. Lizzie had obviously appointed herself an authority on the area, and I was just relieved I'd booked us some relaxing time at the spa.

As the fashion designer in the group, Sarah was going to design and make costumes – at break neck speed – the brief being glamorous Victorian. She'd been doing her part by researching what wealthy young women of the time would have been wearing. She'd taken our measurements at the last get-together and strict instructions had been issued on the subject of not losing or putting on any weight. Updating us regularly on her ideas for each of us, she also had to take account of the weather which could be chilly on the coast at that time of year. Working to a tight timescale she was relying heavily on her loyal and patient staff, already used to her chaotic working style. Our costumes were being sent directly to the hotel, with a trying-on session on our first night over a glass or two of champagne, although I don't think anybody had any doubt that whatever Sarah came up with would be both amazing and unique.

Traffic was slow with, it seemed, a mass exodus to the coast for the weekend, added to which there'd been an accident on the motorway, so my journey took just over six hours. But as I drove through the spectacular estate to reach the hotel, where wild woodland contrasted with pristine manicured gardens, a grand lake house and picturesque small stone cottages, I could feel myself relaxing, and by the time I parked in front of the hotel to be greeted by a parking valet I had a big smile on my face.

Leaving the car keys with him, I ascertained he was also going to arrange for the suitcases to be taken up to my room, and making my way into reception I found Alice and Lizzie ensconced opposite each other on two overstuffed, brightly cushion-covered sofas. I checked in, gratefully accepting a complimentary glass of champagne, and sinking into the cushions next to Alice joined them tucking into dishes of nuts and olives whilst graciously accepting praise for finding this gem of a hotel. Alice pronounced it and the grounds stunning, while Lizzie was amazed I'd managed it all at the last minute. And then Sarah arrived in her usual whirl, adding her enthusiasm to the others. There were bear hugs all round and apparently our costumes had already made it there before us. "Can't wait for you to see them." Sarah knocked back her glass of champagne even quicker than I had, and through a mouthful of olives assured us that should any last-minute minor alterations be needed, she'd brought with her the means to sort them swiftly.

We decided to hit the spa before anything else, and having seen off the plates of snacks, not to mention the champagne, changed and reassembled in the complimentary, luxuriously soft white robes and slippers, which had been laid out on our beds. The verdict was unanimous, the hotel was fabulous, the rooms were gorgeous, and I'd done an amazing job. Things proceeded to get even better, because the hotel brochure had if anything underplayed the spa which was everything you could wish for and more. Deluxe décor, a relaxation room with sinfully comfortable reclining chairs, large heated pool, Jacuzzi, steam room, sauna, and a gym for those so inclined, although I immediately made up my mind that unwinding and restoring was the name of the game for this weekend. In fact, after a wonderful afternoon in the spa ending up in the Jacuzzi, it was as much as we could do to gather in Sarah's room for the big costume reveal, although once we were there, excitement took over. Sarah and her team were super talented and had thrown themselves into the project with enthusiasm. Matching attention to detail with silk, lace and velvet they had surpassed themselves. Our Victorian inspired outfits fitted perfectly and had been designed to suit our individual colouring and style.

My bustled dress was black and blood-red shot silk, trimmed with lace and black velvet. It had a tightly corseted bodice, and wide hooped skirt and even the net underskirt was exquisite. Finishing touches were a full-length black velvet cape, long velvet gloves, and a saucy, small black hat with stiff netting, to partially cover my face. The *pièce de résistance,* presented triumphantly by Sarah to each of us, was an oversized heart necklace and matching earrings in Whitby jet. As we put them on Sarah, fresh from her research, filled us in on the semi-precious stone which apparently had been popularised by Queen Victoria, who spent some time in the area. After the death of Prince Albert, Victoria went into mourning; she wore only black for the rest of her life and jet jewellery caught the imagination of the Victorian public.

I'm ashamed to say, so taken up was I by my incredible transformation with costume and jewellery, that whilst

I could see Alice, Lizzie and Sarah's outfits were equally gorgeous, I spent far more time watching my own reflection, and it was only with great reluctance that I was persuaded to change for a superb dinner in the hotel's restaurant. After dinner we moved on to the bar and spent an enjoyable hour or so toasting our rather radiant bride-to-be, until eyelids started to droop and we agreed a reasonably early night was in order.

The following morning, after a delicious Yorkshire cooked breakfast, and several cups of strong coffee for our mild hangovers, we went up to change. Taking my Gothic makeup instruction from a handy YouTube video I contrasted dark kohl around my eyes, false eyelashes and dark eyebrows with much lighter foundation, a dramatic slash of blusher and a combination of deep red and black lipstick. As a final Gothic touch I added a small black mole above my lip before hurrying down to meet the others. I think we were all momentarily stunned at how easily we'd slipped from the 21st century into another era. I suppose the only clouds on our horizon were the restrictions we weren't used to; sharply nipped in waists, tight bodices and who knew a bustle would be so uncomfortable? Despite that, none of us were going to complain, Sarah had gone to endless trouble, but it did make me think twice about those genuine Victorians who'd dressed this way daily.

Our taxi arrived dead on time with the driver not turning a hair as we took our time climbing in – a bustle not being the easiest thing to handle in a car packed like sardines – and we guessed he must be well used to the town going mad at festival time. Dropped on the east side of town, first stop was historic Church Street, already crowded with a host of ghost-like figures strolling the uneven cobbles, and Sarah, her research providing authority, pointed out the differences between Steampunks, Cybergoths, and those dressed Victorian-style like us.

We joined the throng. I was arm in arm with Alice, and Lizzie with Sarah which we all agreed laughing was as much for balance on the cobbles as for affection. The many bistros and cafés had taken full advantage of the sunshine with outside tables and chairs, and people were already happily eating and drinking. As we continued down the main street, we peered into narrow passages widening into yards and spotted several drinkers sneaking an early pint at the mariner's inns.

The atmosphere was heady – from a quaint shop with tiny doors and Georgian cross windows, wafted scents of herbs and incense, while from another, roasted coffee and freshly baked bread. These blended as we moved and mixed with the tempting heavenly perfume from a handmade soap store. Bookshop windows were full of *Dracula*, *The Whitby Witches* and other equally alarming Gothic tales, and were draped in spiders' webs and populated with an assortment of spiders and bats. We'd totally underestimated the numbers of people who'd turned out for the festival and commented again how lucky we'd been to be able to book the hotel at such a late date.

The costumes we saw were outstanding and Alice and I kept bumping into Lizzie and Sarah in front of us because

Sarah was totally distracted by what she was seeing. It would seem people went to extraordinary lengths, time and money no object, to achieve the perfect look. This was escapism at its finest. Many of the women were dressed as were we, in glamorous Gothic style, black net, shimmering velvet and vivid black and red silks. Hats with sweeping feathers topped white-foundationed faces, startlingly slashed with black or scarlet lipstick, and nobody had held back on the eye makeup. The men weren't to be outdone, with long black funereal overcoats which swept the ground as they walked, opening to reveal crushed velvet waistcoats in striking shades of deep burgundy and dark green. Shiny black shoes, top hats and skull-headed walking canes made for an elegant stride from some, whilst others had donned helmets with horns, like the original Goths, or opted for graphic plague, or unnerving crow's head masks.

Those who'd gone totally *Pirates of the Caribbean* with large black hats and dreadlocks mingled easily with the Steampunk brigade, top hats adorned with brass goggles and guns. Whitby wasn't so much stepping back in time, as hurling itself into its Gothic past. Alice squeezed my arm with excitement, and we grinned at each other; this was an incredible experience and there was a fabulous vibe, people stopping strangers to exclaim, admire or compare outfits.

By the time we'd reached Arguments Yard it was flattering to find that with all the competition, our group seemed much in demand both by professional photographers covering the event and by other festival-goers, their wielded phones anachronistic against their outfits. There was another photo opportunity as we moved on, to stand in front of a huge spider in the middle of a web on the wall of Hamond's the jewellers. It was disconcerting though to find ourselves alongside a kilted, elderly chap with a long white beard. He was manacled, wailing loudly and rattling the thick iron chain looped through the manacles and secured by a large iron ring set into the ground, but we were reassured when he gave us a big grin and a wink before resuming the wailing.

There was no time for shopping, but I couldn't resist a peek in the shop window, because these were the original jet-black precious stone specialists, and looking around me I could see how popular Whitby jet had become once again with partygoers sporting impressive necklaces and oversize rings. I promised myself I'd return and take a better look when the crowds died down, I was sure I'd find a beautiful piece or two.

We walked as far as the first of the 199 Steps, and decided, feet starting to ache in unfamiliar shoes and sore from cobble negotiating, that we'd save the steps for the next day. Turning we started to make our way back, spotting things we'd originally missed – a wonderfully Gothic yard by the old church building, a wrought iron archway decorated with black ribbons, beads, and fairy lights. Whitby was so far removed from the high street in Richmond with its designer clothes, coffee shops, and wine bars. Everyone around me had a real smile on their face, and the enjoyment in the air was tangible. It wasn't a huge stretch of the imagination to think of the Victorians, as we walked where they'd walked. I could see them parading, purchasing jet jewellery, taking tea at the quaint tea rooms, which even today used vintage china cups and saucers. Maybe they would have bought humbugs and liquorice root at the sweet shops, or taken themselves to one of the inns off the main street for a drink. I chuckled to myself; there was no doubt I'd fallen hook, line and sinker for the magical vibe of Whitby.

We spent a pleasurable afternoon back at the hotel relaxing and enjoying a massage, before getting back into costume and heading off for an early dinner. Lizzie had booked a restaurant on Skinner Street. It was a delightful French restaurant, with rave reviews. Food, ambience, and service were fantastic and enjoyed all the more because we'd discovered we were ravenous. We tucked in with a vengeance despite the restrictions of corseted clothing and agreed we'd walk it off when we headed for the Music Festival. We'd been a little unsure about this particular event and as feared it was deafening, with a pounding bass that made it impossible to either make out the song or have any conversation. I don't think I was the only one with a throbbing head, and we all agreed to beat a hasty retreat to a small mariner's inn in one of the yards for a quiet drink before the Ghost Walk Lizzie had arranged for us at 9.00.

We met our guide, Dr Will Sutcliffe, as prearranged in the marketplace, just off Church Street. As he shook our hands and we made introductions, he charmingly clarified he wasn't of the medical persuasion, but had done his PhD on paranormal activities in Whitby and on the Yorkshire

Moors. He'd become so fascinated, almost obsessed he said with a wry grin, by what he found that having completed his doctorate, he simply carried on researching, funding being well provided for by his private tour guide work.

In shiny funereal top hat, long black overcoat and boots laced to the knee he was dressed as a Victorian undertaker, and it had to be said, looked decidedly sinister. Nevertheless we exchanged approving looks behind his back. With his curly long black hair, dark brooding looks, olive skin, and deep brown eyes enhanced with black eye makeup he was rather gorgeous, and Lizzie murmured in my ear he could come and scare her anytime! He reminded me of a rugged Johnny Depp, and he certainly knew his stuff; his knowledge of both the history and paranormal activity of Whitby was vast and he was easily able to answer all the questions we fired at him, and as we moved around the town, his stories were mesmerising.

We learnt about the elephants the Maharaja, a guest of Queen Victoria, kept at the nearby Mulgrave Estate, often parading them on the beach in Whitby. He suggested we listen carefully, as on dark nights they could sometimes still be heard, a ghostly trumpeting of grief at their loss of freedom. He told us about the 19th-century landlady of the White Horse and Griffin Public House, a particularly spiteful and unpleasant individual who loathed most of her customers, and never held back in saying so. One night she slipped and cracked her head. She called for help, but no-one came and she suffered a long, slow solitary death on the cold cobbles. "Should you go into one of her inns," Will said, "and start to feel uneasy, get out quickly – the landlady may have taken a dislike to you and bad luck will follow."

Grape Lane had originally been Grope Lane – the red light district – and naturally there was a story there too. In those days people made their own loaves and took them along to the baker to be baked. One baker, too lazy to get up, let a young girl place her loaf into the huge oven, and only when he heard bloodcurdling screams, did he turn his head to see her engulfed in flames. Sadly she died of her injuries, and it is said she now haunts Grape Lane, as a fearsome and flaming apparition.

After an hour or so, with all the information, our heads were aching as much as our feet so we invited Will to join us for a drink, although we didn't let him off the hook, the more questions he answered, the more we kept asking. He told us about the Whitby Museum in Pannett Park, where the Hand of Glory was kept, explaining this was a dried pickled hand of a man who'd been hanged. It was meant to have magical properties, although we laughed at that, the fact he'd been hanged didn't seem to indicate any magic would be for the good.

When we parted from Will at the end of the evening, it was in the certain knowledge that he had evoked in us an unexpected passion for ghosts, spooky stories, and a huge desire to know more.

So eager were we to explore this newfound interest that even Sarah was on time when we met up on our second day, and headed back to The Ropery, Grape Lane, and other narrow cobbled streets we'd discovered the night before. When we got out of the taxi we spotted two guys who were attracting a good deal of attention, and they certainly put smiles on our faces. One had set himself up somewhere between a Goth and a Steampunk sporting a short, deep-purple and black tutu, with a white net underskirt over sheer black tights, and heavy Doc Marten boots. He'd tied a black and white skull-decorated scarf round his waist beneath a black lace jacket and hadn't stinted on the jewellery either. In addition to an impressive Rolex he had a sizeable black-jet ring, and huge, hooped earrings. To these he'd added deep red lipstick and a lace eye-mask, topped with a dashingly wide, lace decorated black hat. You might have assumed he'd draw the line there, but you'd be wrong; for good measure he was wielding a sheer lace umbrella. His friend was a little more on the conservative side, in a long black coat with velvet trimmed pockets and lapels worn over tight black leather trousers. Beneath a funereal top hat brightened by iridescent blue peacock feathers, he had on gold-rimmed glasses, Steampunk style and for good measure – always good to have a spare – another pair tucked into the rim of the hat. They'd stopped to let a photographer take some shots, black coat man smiled and waved beringed fingers while his friend winked and lifted the net skirt to reveal a cheeky lacy black and white garter.

We finally stopped in Henrietta Street for a moment or two to get our breath back and admire the view across the harbour where, amidst sailing, speed and fishing boats, bobbed the bright orange RNLI lifeboat. There was also a pleasure boat taking revellers round the harbour – we could hear the excited chatter and laughter from where we stood. Then our attention was diverted by a replica pirate ship, its Jolly Roger skull and crossbones flag flying, which was also sailing around the harbour to cheers from observers.

The delicious smell of smoked kippers from Fortunes Smokehouse was starting to make us feel hungry. So we headed towards the 199 steps up to St Mary's Church and on to the ancient clifftop abbey, although making our way through the crowd wasn't easy. We passed a tiny cottage where apparently coffins had been stored before being taken up to the church, and mercifully as we climbed we could see benches at regular intervals. Originally built for breathless pallbearers to stop and take a rest on the way up, they did equally well for modern day visitors. Smiling at the others, I could see they were feeling much the same as me. I'd never been anywhere where there was so much magic and energy in the air, and I was surprised by the sudden, intense wave of emotion I felt.

By this time though, sightseeing done, our feet in their beautiful shoes were starting to ache a fair bit, and it was agreed we'd slowly start making our way back. Alice pointed out that superbly fitted as our dresses were, they didn't really lend themselves to a steep climb and deep breaths, which is why we were all making do with short pants! We were helping each other down the steep steps and still laughing at that, when with no warning, something indescribable happened.

A sudden crackle of electrical energy hit the air, and I could feel stray strand ends of my hair pulling away from my head, while the other-worldly glow of the sun gave the harbour below me an unsettling, strangely sepia appearance; it was eerie. My surroundings became blurred, although looking straight ahead I could see with complete clarity the drastically different change in the harbour traffic. Old-fashioned clipper sailing ships, and fishing boats of different sizes moved on the water, nothing like the contemporary crafts of a moment earlier. The lighthouse and pier had completely disappeared, and turning my head slowly I looked inland to where, around the east side, smoke was snaking into the clear sky from terracotta chimney pots atop the fishermen's cottages surrounding the harbour.

There was a buzz of noise and activity; white-bonneted women with woollen shawls over long skirts and hessian aprons were working hard picking and putting items from the base of the cliffs into large wicker baskets, some of which were carried, perfectly balanced on their heads.

At the same time men on the beach were labouring over torn fishing nets or carrying lobster pots from the boats, good-naturedly jeering at those taking a break to smoke clay pipes. And there were a dozen or so children of assorted age and size. With grubby laughing faces and tattered clothing, they were weaving in and out of the adults in a game of tag, batted good-naturedly aside when they got in the way. The smell of burning wood, roasting meat and smoked fish was all around me, overlaid now and then with the far sweeter scents of lavender and rosemary wafting my way with the breeze. And then there was a sudden, unmistakeable, nose-wrinkling pungent stench of urine, and I retched. As I did, the scene before me lost its clarity, became blurred and indistinct, then everything went completely black.

CHAPTER 4

There was something cold chilling my forehead, and I forced open my reluctant eyelids to see Alice, frowning and worried, bending over me with tissues which she was dampening from a bottle of water. I was lying on one of the old wooden benches alongside the path, the ones set there for pallbearers and coffins I recalled ruefully, as I struggled to sit up.

Lizzie and Sarah were fronting a crowd of concerned and curious onlookers, and Alice was patting my hand. "Ellie, can you hear me? Sweetie, you went down like a pack of cards, what on earth happened?" Lizzie put her arm around my shoulders, as I sat up so I was leaning against her, and glad of the support.

"Shush, Alice," she said firmly, "Let her catch her breath," and she held another bottle of water to my lips. "Sip slowly." Sarah, pale with shock, was wringing her hands.

"My fault," she wailed, "It's my fault, I made your costume too tight. Look, we've undone the zip now, and I'll put in a couple of safety pins later, to hold it. You should have said something." I smiled and shook my head, relieved the dress was definitely looser now.

"Not your fault, don't be silly." I took a couple of deep breaths, and glanced quickly over towards the harbour, my heart thumping. But normal seemed to have made a come-back. The clipper ships, and the fishermen's boats had disappeared along with the men and women in their sack-like clothing, and there was no sign either of the ragged kids with snotty noses and dirty clothes, only the same holidaymakers and festivalgoers I was used to seeing.

Out on the water the pirate ship was still circling, the crowd in the pleasure ship still making a racket, the orange lifeboat was again bobbing up and down by the lifeboat station. Thankfully, also gone was the overpowering stench of urine, replaced now by the aroma of fish and chips and vinegar blended in the salty sea air. But it had been so real, I could recall exactly how the sky had changed colour, the electrical charge in the air, followed by the crystal clarity of the scene, complete with sounds and smells – a clean, clear window into the past. Could it all have been a figment of my over-heated imagination?

Looking at the worried faces of my friends, I made a swift decision. I wouldn't say anything, it would sound totally crazy. They'd laugh at me, blaming the ghost stories with which we'd been regaled the previous evening, but they'd worry nevertheless. "I must have fainted," I said, "One minute I was looking out at the harbour, next thing everything went black." "You did look pale, a bit spaced out," Alice agreed, "But before I could say anything, you were flat out. Lucky you didn't hit your head."

"Might have knocked a bit of sense into her," Lizzie said, then went serious again. "How do you feel? You were out cold for what seemed like ages." She paused, "You're not ..?"

"Not what?" asked Alice, and I laughed, "No, definitely not. I just felt a fit of the vapours was called for, so I could say I was being authentically Victorian. Honestly, I'm OK now, sorry, everyone, you must have had an awful fright. But I'm fine, let's get on, we've things to see."

I wasn't being strictly truthful; there was an odd tingling sensation in my head, a tight knot in the pit of my stomach and my fingers for some reason were oddly wrinkled at the ends, as if I'd stayed overlong in the bath. I slipped my gloves on quickly. The last thing I wanted was for anyone to notice and start asking questions to which I didn't have any answers. I nodded enthusiastically when Sarah suggested that perhaps our next stop should be somewhere we could boost our energy levels, recover our equilibrium, and perhaps partake of a small glass of wine – obviously only for the shock. Alice remembered she'd spotted a cute bistro in one of the yards we'd passed, and we were delighted to find it had an outside seating area.

"Perfect," declared Lizzie as we settled ourselves at a large wooden table, with brightly cushioned chairs. The sun was warm in this sheltered corner of the lush courtyard where we were surrounded by rustic wooden plant boxes, tight-packed with vivid, jewel-coloured spring flowers, evergreens and topiary. The fragrance of the spring blooms blended with the coffee and garlic wafting from the bistro inside. Lizzie went to the bar to order, and we three sat in companionable silence for a few moments, glad of a rest after the earlier alarm, although of course the others had no idea of the extent of it – to be honest, neither did I. I thought it best to put it all aside to consider later and just enjoy where I was now. An early bumble bee was bumbling productively from bloom to bloom, taking advantage of the unseasonable weather, and I focused on the pleasing hum of different conversations, picking up on the odd phrase here, or laugh there as the sounds rose and fell amidst the clatter of crockery and cutlery.

Lizzie returned to the table, mission accomplished while a cheerfully flushed waitress came to set the table and assure us our food and drinks would be with us shortly. Sarah was first to break the silence, "Better, Ellie?" I could see she was still blaming herself. I squeezed her hand, "I'm fine, nothing a bite to eat and a glass of vino won't fix, sorry I made a bit of an exhibition of myself."

"Well you always were a drama queen," Lizzie observed, "but your colour's better, you looked ghastly before." I joined in the laughter, but was desperate to steer the chat away from me. "Don't you all feel part of something special? I've never experienced anything like it, I absolutely love it here!"

"I know you all would have preferred somewhere hot," said Alice a little smugly, "But I bet you're glad we're here now, I know I am." Her tone changed and she leaned forward a little. "You do know you're the best friends a girl could have, and I can't thank you enough for organising all this." Uncharacteristically for Alice, she was tearing up. I knew if she went, the rest of us would too and it could turn into a tissue fest. I broke the moment with, "Well you can't say I haven't jumped right into the spirit of things."

"Indeed," Sarah muttered, "and nearly gave us a heart attack in the process." We laughed, and then chilled white wine, hummus, olives, and pitta bread arrived and we all dived right in.

We took our time over lunch, then called a taxi back to the hotel. The others decided to go for a stroll through the grounds, while I opted to head up to my room. Truth was, I couldn't wait to change out of the costume, but didn't want to appear ungrateful in front of Sarah after all her hard work. It was certainly stunning and I loved it, but it was without a doubt the most uncomfortable thing I'd ever worn, and only when I changed into some comfortable loungewear did I relax a little. The luxuriously deep down-quilt, immaculate on the bed, was calling to me. I didn't resist, and pausing only to set the alarm on my phone to wake me an hour later was asleep before my head hit the pillow.

***

Walking through the rickety gate, I notice it's nearly falling off its hinges. I close it carefully. The stone cottage is ahead, sitting in its own grounds. No sign of anyone, the only sound the tinkling of the babbling brook, counterpointed by harsh screeches from rooks settling on the roof. Smoke curls from the chimney so someone's in. As I move forward I smell the scent from deep purple lavender and rosemary, abundant in the wild, overgrown garden along with other herbs and vegetables all battling for space with entwined weeds and wildflowers wrapping around them. My feet don't feel as if they're touching the ground, yet I move swift and sure down the cobbled path. There is sadness, neglect and disrepair in the paint peeling from the front door, over which a sprig of dried moorland heather tied with old bootlaces is balanced across two farrier's nails. Above the doorframe is a Y-shaped branch.

Rusted garden tools were discarded either side of the path, and a battered wicker basket, brimming with what looked like foraging spoils was on the doorstep. It held mushrooms of all shapes and sizes from tiny and grey to large and white, and on the top of the pile was a disconcertingly saucer-sized, speckled-top specimen. There were also twigs, berries, and an assortment of herbs, their scent under-laid by that of fresh earth. A feeling of great calm overtook me, and without thinking I found myself opening the door, taking care to push it a little harder at the point where it always stuck – and before I'd had a chance to think that through, I was in a warm, farmhouse kitchen, its flagstone floor scattered with sawdust.

There was no surprise on the face of the young woman who turned to greet me with a smile of welcome. I'd say she was in her mid-twenties, around my build, with a tanned face innocent of makeup and exuberantly long dark hair, controlled by a band of white flowers. As she moved towards me, blue eyes sparkling with pleasure, the scent of the flowers was exquisitely familiar to me. She wore a simple, threadbare full-length grey skirt under a stained and torn in places hessian pinafore, and scratches on her arms and face bore testimony to the foraging involved in gathering the goodies in the basket outside.

She held out her hands to take mine after a momentary hesitation, I let her. "Ellie, we've been expecting you," she said, "Welcome to our home, I am Hettie." With my hands in hers, reality crept back in and I tried to take a step back. What the heck was happening here? She maintained her gentle hold.

"Who are you?" I said, "How do you know my name? I don't understand." And now, close to her, I understood even less – her blue eyes were the ones I saw every day in my mirror. "You ... you look like me," I said, and was aware that had come out in a somewhat accusatory tone. She smiled, "Ellie, please don't be alarmed, you are here for a reason." And oddly enough, such was her warmth and certainty I relaxed a little.

It was only then I saw we weren't alone. An older, white-bonneted woman was supervising the contents of a large pot suspended over the open fire; she was busy peeling vegetables from a pile on the nearby table and adding them to whatever was cooking, and it smelt delicious. Watching her was a child, about five years old I thought. She was concentrating intently on cramming as many blackberries as she could into her mouth, deep purple staining hands, lips, and what might once have been a clean white pinafore. The room was smoky from the fire and gloomy, because a couple of candles on the windowsill and another on the table were the only source of lighting. Maybe there was a power cut. But glancing around I couldn't see any lighting fixtures, so perhaps this family was one of the 'back to nature, save the planet' types. I felt a little like Alice in Wonderland, in a strange yet familiar land, then I gave a start and took a step back as I saw what looked like a shrivelled hand on one of the windowsills. Black with age, it was serving as a candle holder. I recalled Will's explanation from our tour. It was a Hand of Glory, keeping the household safe from harm, nevertheless I looked away quickly, and as she caught my eye, the child crammed a few more berries into an already full mouth and moved to hang on to Hettie's skirt, her blackberry juice-covered fingers staining the material she touched. She contemplated me solemnly through long, tangled dark brown hair which hadn't seen a brush recently – if ever. She was a beautiful child, with a dusting of freckles on her sun-kissed face, and startlingly blue eyes. "My daughter, Bessie," Hettie told me, and nodding her head at the woman, "My mother, Agnes – Aggie to us." The woman looked up with a brief smile and inclination of the head before turning attention back to the vegetables.

Bessie, apparently feeling she'd done her social duty, wandered back to her grandmother who started singing softly, suiting the rhythm of the song to the peeling of an enormous carrot she was tackling, and after a moment the child joined in, and they exchanged smiles as their voices blended. It was close to a tune I remembered from my own childhood. Smiling, our hands still linked, Hettie pulled me gently towards a roughly-made wooden settle where two threadbare seat cushions seemed to have lost most of their straw stuffing through a rip on the side. She removed another basket full of forest findings and guided me with a slight downward pressure of her hand so that I took a seat. It was just as uncomfortable as it looked.

"I am so thankful you finally found me." Hettie said, and in response to my look of total bafflement added, "There is much to explain, but you must be patient." I shook my head; things, as so often happens in a dream, were not becoming one jot clearer. "I need to teach you," she said, "But we don't have a lot of time."

I shook my head again. "Sorry," I said, "Still not with you."

She continued as if I hadn't spoken, her tone urgent. "Listen carefully, I have been reaching out to you all your life, you are my lost soul. I know you have seen my demise since you were a child, but there's so much I need to teach you before I go. I've waited so long for you to come, at times I even doubted you would." A tear rolled down her cheek, and she wiped it briskly on the stained pinafore.

"I have absolutely no idea what you're talking about," I said. I was concerned at her distress, but even in my dream state I was pretty convinced I was dealing with possible mental health issues here. Taking in her appearance as we sat, I shivered; I could have been looking in a mirror at what-might-have-been me without the makeup and expensive grooming.

"They are coming for me, and I feel it won't be long." She still had hold of my hands, and leaning forward had lowered her tone so much that instinctively I leaned forward too, so I could hear her better. "You have seen how they extinguish my earthly existence; you've seen that since you were a small child, seen me drown, time and again." I pulled my hands abruptly from hers, shaken to the core – my nightmare, how could she know? She saw my reaction and nodded, "Your task now is to learn, whilst there is still time." She rested her head wearily for a moment against the unforgiving wooden back of the settle. "You are the only one who can understand, you will become my voice, and the guardian of the truth."

I fought a wave of nausea that suddenly hit me with the realisation it wasn't me. All the years of nightmares, it wasn't me drowning, it was Hettie. I hadn't spoken but she answered me. "Indeed, Ellie, you have been seeing and feeling what I will feel. I am your past life. You must take the learning from me and carry it forward to your own time," she smiled. "You will soon realise you already know so much; it is part of you, ingrained in your heart and soul. But, Ellie, you have been ignoring your calling, and that has made you unhappy." I was shaking my head vehemently even as what she was saying was shedding light on my feelings of unfulfilment and dissatisfaction.

"You need to learn quickly." Her voice was low but that didn't disguise the urgency. "This knowledge must not die with me. They will come for me in the autumn." I started to shake uncontrollably, swamped with anxiety; this was a watershed moment, and I needed a few seconds before I could respond, and when I did, nothing else but the truth would do, I'd seen the trees painted red and gold, felt the chill of coming winter. "I know," I said then, "I've seen and felt it over and over, is there nothing that can be done to stop it?" She shook her head.

"You must understand, you cannot stop this from happening, there are dark forces and they are so powerful." She took a breath and went on, "I am being persecuted by the villagers, accused of things I have not done. Anything that goes wrong is my fault – milk curdles, crop won't take, a cow dies or there is a stillborn child – blame is laid nowhere else but at my door, I am the scapegoat." I started to say something but she held up a restraining hand. "The persecution of women for witchcraft is now against the law of the land, but that won't change things, won't stop the zealots, won't stop those steeped in the old ways. They will try me as a witch and there will be no voice raised in my defence. And as is the way of the village, they will close ranks; even those that don't agree with what is happening will turn a blind eye." She was speaking lower and faster now; she didn't want the child to hear. I had to move closer and concentrate harder on what she was saying. "Ellie, I have a wealth of knowledge as you will soon see, knowledge handed down through the generations. I have only ever used it for good, have helped so many with my lotions, my herb potions and yes, my spells. I have nothing to be ashamed of, but one by one people have been turned from me, and the truth of the matter is that the men lead a witch hunt, the others who go along with it proclaim themselves God's Hand, doing God's work. Maybe they even convince themselves, but the pleasure they get from the fear, pain and death of a woman is all-encompassing."

She paused, but when I opened my mouth to speak, rushed on, "Passing my magic to you is essential. You can't save me but if I awaken the witch in you, the old knowledge will not die. I have concealed what you need in a safe place, so back in your world you will be able to make sense of what you need to do, you will use what I give you wisely as I have always done."

I pulled away from her, and was able finally to speak, my head spinning – this was so crazy I didn't know what to say and indeed, the first words out of my mouth, were crazy too. "How will I find what you're hiding?" then I said something a little more sensible, "Nothing you can teach me could be used in my time." I shrugged, "My world is unlike yours, things have moved on, there's no place for what you're talking about." Hettie's smile was knowing, and a little bitter.

"There will never be a time when such knowledge is not needed, it is there, dear Ellie, it is always there, you just haven't recognised it for what it is. But all will become clear, you already have so much within you, it is in our blood, mine and yours and we will use that power in your time. We are not able to change our destiny, but we can learn from it. This is a time of massive change for you."

I shook my head again. "No, you're wrong, I'm not making any changes and I really have no idea what you're talking about." She smiled again, this time more genuinely amused.

"Ellie, even when I am not around, the window into my time has been opened, it cannot be closed now, you will be able to step through whenever you have need. Deep inside, you know this to be true." I nodded reluctantly; she wasn't wrong, outlandish and impossible as this all seemed, nevertheless there was no doubting the solidity of the wooden settle beneath me, the warmth of her breath as she spoke, the crackling of the wood in the fireplace.

"But," she went on, "I must warn you, there will be many who cannot or will not understand your calling, and whilst you will find others of our kind, always watch for those who want to do you harm, wolves in sheep's clothing. You will meet your soulmate, but take care because not everyone is what they seem and everything carries its own risks."

Her voice was starting to fade and whilst I could see her mouth moving she was being drowned out by a persistent loud knocking, I turned to look at Aggie; why wasn't she answering the door? I tried to ask, but found I could no longer speak. And then I heard someone screaming my name, "Ellie, Ellie, open the door, are you OK? Please open the door." Still enmeshed in the dream, God it had been so real, I jumped out of bed. It was Lizzie at the door, and for a moment, one foot still in the cottage, I smiled; what might Lizzie have thought if Aggie had opened the door instead of me? Of course it was only a dream but at that moment Hettie, Aggie and the child were more real, more tangibly alive in my mind than my anxious friend demanding to be let in.

CHAPTER 5

I knew I needed to put on a pretty good act to distract the girls from their concern. Lizzie having almost battered the door down last night to wake me when I hadn't turned up for dinner, I'd slept through the alarm. We knew each other so well, and they knew something wasn't quite right with me, so they were seriously worried. So much so that like a group of anxious mothers, when Lizzie finally brought me downstairs they'd ganged up to insist that as soon as we got back I must make an appointment to get myself checked out. "Preferably," said Alice, brooking no argument, "With a specialist! And don't think for one moment we'll stop nagging until you do."

"OK, Mum," I'd agreed, laughing, "If it will make you happy, but I'm telling you I'm just tired – and right now I'm starving, so give me a break and let's order."

I was mortified to be causing my best friends so much worry and could only imagine their conversations when I wasn't there. I was determined Alice would have the best time ever for the remainder of her hen weekend, which meant I had to nix any more drama. By the time we'd finished our main course and were relaxing over an utterly delicious and sinfully chocolate-laden dessert, we were chatting and laughing as normal, and the mere fact that they were reassured made me feel a lot better too.

My sleep that night was wonderfully dreamless, with Hettie, thank goodness, nowhere to be seen, and I woke refreshed and ready to take a far more prosaic view. In all likelihood, the weird Whitby happenings were simply down to me having worked my socks off over the last few months without a break. I knew I'd been pretty exhausted when I left London, it was my overworked imagination running wild with my overworked body following suit. As for Hettie and family, well we all know dreams can sometimes seem more real than reality; although there was the possibility Hettie, figment of my imagination though she might have been, was actually my subconscious trying to tell me something. I resolved that when I had a moment, I'd jot down everything I remembered of the dream. The main thing now was to enjoy the rest of the time with my friends and avoid scaring them silly any more than I had already.

Feeling far more my usual practical self and in control of things, I was ready for the day ahead. Jumping out of bed and gritting my teeth against the chill, I gave myself a quick blast in a cold shower before hiking up the temperature – apparently it opened the pores and was good for you, and I hoped that was true because it was hell to do. Encasing myself in the gratifyingly large and luxurious bath sheet, I noticed some flaking on my arms and legs; maybe too much time in the sun, although I had been covered up most of the time, still it wouldn't do. I slathered on a generous amount of my rich (ridiculously priced) body cream, special attention paid to the dry patches and while that was absorbed, brushed my still wet hair. It felt dryer and more brittle than usual – my fault, I hadn't bothered to get out my own rich shampoo and conditioner, had just used what the hotel supplied, serve me right. I'd wash it properly again before dinner tonight.

Looking into the bathroom mirror, my face didn't look great either, the lighting like the bath sheets was top notch and showed rather more than I wanted to see, a grey-tinted pallor. As I hastily reached for foundation that promised a 'healthy, natural glow', I could only hope it lived up to its word. I must have been more tired than I thought. My daily night and morning beauty regime was meticulous, nourishing my skin was as important as cleaning my teeth, surely a couple of days away from my usual routine wouldn't have had this dramatic impact?

I was starting to feel anxious again; my fingers were tingling and looking at them I could see they were still wrinkled like prunes; what was happening to me? Maybe it was something to do with being near the sea, all that salt? When I got back to London there was a Knightsbridge beauty salon, exclusive and eye-wateringly expensive, who'd be hearing from me. On my way to the wardrobe, I pulled aside the curtain for a peek at typical British spring weather. The temperature had dropped from yesterday's glorious sunshine, there were some grey clouds and it looked as if it could rain. Lizzie had organised a guided walking trip this morning, a novelty for me, couldn't remember the last time I had been on this type of trip, probably not since school, and I hadn't the faintest idea what to wear so called Alice who always got it right for every occasion.

She answered, immediately worried. "Ellie, what's wrong?"

"Nothing, silly, told you, was just tired yesterday and it was only meant to be a power nap. I feel fantastic today, but you have to help – what do I wear for this trip?"

"Layers," she said firmly, "Layers always work, you can put on or take off according to hot or cold. I brought a waterproof jacket, and walking boots, have you ..."

I interrupted, "Certainly have. Thanks, Alice, just needed a clue."

"Off you go then, rifle through your country casuals, I'll see you downstairs." She sounded relieved and I felt guilty all over again about giving them grief. I pulled on my skinny jeans, a long sleeved t-shirt, brand new blush pink cashmere jumper, and even had a rucksack into which I put a waterproof jacket and water bottle. I left all that with my walking boots by the door so I could dash up and get them after breakfast. I grinned at my reflection in one of the many mirrors around the room. I have to confess, I was rather impressed that having been pointed in the right direction by Alice, I actually had everything to hand. My reflection grinned back and then suddenly I shivered, odd because it was if anything too warm in the room. For goodness sake, if I was going to see everything as ominous I'd drive myself mad. I shook off my uneasiness and headed downstairs.

***

As we lined up on the porticoed steps of the hotel, waiting for our guide, Lizzie was just explaining that we were going to start at Runswick Bay and walk the Cleveland way to Whitby, when a 4 x 4 Land Cruiser belted up the drive and drew to a gravel-raising stop in front of us. It was a vehicle which had seen better days, a lot of them obviously muddy, and there were enough dents and scrapes to indicate that the speed with which it had arrived was par for the course. Alice's expression of horror was echoed by Lizzie's of panic as, coughing to hide a laugh, I put my head down and followed Sarah, who was obviously less concerned about mud than the rest of us, into the back of the vehicle.

The outside should perhaps have prepared us for the number of discarded apple cores, sweet wrappers, and empty crisp packets on the inside, not to mention the dog hairs on the back seat and the extremely strange smell emanating from the back of the vehicle where we'd dumped our bags. I wasn't sure I even wanted to know what the smell was, sometimes ignorance is better. Our guide Steph, whatever the state of her transport, greeted us warmly. We knew from Lizzie she'd been a head teacher in a previous career, and semi-retired now subsidised her income as an artist by leading guided tours a couple of times a week.

"OK, ladies," she said as we climbed in, "Make yourselves comfortable, we're off to Runswick Bay to start our walk. When we end in Whitby, I'm going to suggest you take a taxi back to the hotel or," she added with a broad wink at Lizzie in the passenger seat next to her, "You can walk, if you think you'll have the energy!" She sniggered. We all laughed too, and I felt Alice relax a little and good-naturedly resign herself to this not being the sort of transport she'd have chosen given the chance.

Steph obviously wasn't prepared to modify her driving for the comfort of passengers. Lizzie had grabbed a strap above the passenger side door and was hanging on grimly while Sarah, Alice and I for lack of anything else were hanging on, equally grimly, to each other. Steph seemed to take each steep hill as a personal challenge. I never suffer from travel sickness but there was definitely a moment or two when I thought my breakfast might be about to make a reappearance. I didn't dare look at the others, and we were all unusually silent except for the odd little squeak of panic from Alice. Luckily Steph, who appeared totally oblivious to the dire state of her 4x4, the awful odour and her nervous and stressed passengers, had a great deal to say.

Our stopping point was the car park at the base of the steep hill which dropped sharply into Runswick Bay, although Steph didn't seem to feel it necessary to slow down at all for this. As we hurtled down, Alice squeezed my hand so tightly I thought I might never get back the use of my fingers. It was a huge relief when we swung wildly into the car park and screeched to a halt. Exiting on somewhat wobbly legs I think we were all thinking thank God there wouldn't be a return journey, and I could hear Lizzie muttering to no-one in particular, "Eight-mile walk? No problem."

Determined to put our dramatic journey behind me I took out my phone to focus instead on the breathtaking scenery in front of us. The others had strolled on, so I was the only one standing with Steph when she hauled one of those professional walking sticks beloved by hikers from the back of the car, tutting as it got caught on something. Glancing over I must have exclaimed out loud, as what had entangled with the stick seemed to be a dead cat. Steph looked over her shoulder. "Mildred," she said in explanation.

"Is it...she dead?" What a daft question, I'm no animal expert but this was definitely a cat that was no longer with us, and hadn't been for some time, no wonder there was a stench.

Steph wrinkled her nose a little as she delivered the understatement of the year, "Bit smelly now, probably kept her too long." I nodded. I shouldn't judge, maybe a beloved pet, but before I could express sympathy, she added, "Been using her for artwork, no good alive, they move too much."

"Right," I said faintly as she locked the 4x4 – although I'm not sure who'd have dreamt of stealing it – and slipped into tour guide or maybe it was headmistress mode, as we caught up with the others. She gestured towards the phones we were all holding. "Won't need those, girls, I'm happy to take pictures for you, so you can focus on your feet and the scenery." We all nodded, thinking that seemed like a sensible idea. I passed her my phone deciding it would do no-one any good to mention Mildred, and we dutifully if cautiously fell into step as she led the way down the steep winding path leading onto the beach. Once there, we were buffeted by the stiff north east breeze, and Steph beckoned us closer. "That's it, girls, gather round, otherwise you won't hear a word." She raised her voice against the wind and the crashing waves, and began, "As you may know, this is an area steeped in myth and folklore, Runswick Bay particularly has a rich history, have you heard of the Hobs?" We shook our heads, "Well, take a look around you, can you spot all those tiny holes in the cliffs? They're known locally as Hob Holes." She deepened her tone; taking school assemblies over the years had presumably taught her how to hold an audience. "Hobs are shaggy-haired, goblin-like creatures, and ..." she paused and indicated, "these holes are where they live. Sometimes though, one or two Hobs break away, and move out to attach themselves to a local farming family – and they're made very welcome, because they take on all sorts of tasks to help around the farm."

"Ooh, I could do with one of those at home," Lizzie put in.

"Sounds as if you are expecting one to pop a head out any minute," Sarah joked. We laughed. Steph didn't, she continued as if Sarah hadn't spoken.

"They're shy creatures, they've been sighted from the top of the cliff, but try and get a picture and you'll find they've disappeared deep into the caves again." None of us was completely certain whether she was being funny, and if she wasn't, it really wouldn't do to laugh again.

Alice, thank goodness, stepped in with a question. "What exactly did they do for the families, Steph?" "Oh, anything that was needed, farm work or in the house. Sensitive though, the Hobs, very sensitive indeed and easily upset, especially if they were not appreciated."

"Sounds like every cleaner I've ever had," Lizzie couldn't resist.

Sarah, though, was caught up in the tale, "So what? They up and leave if you offend them?"

"Sometimes. Sometimes they stay." Steph let a dramatic beat pass before adding, "And then they could be truly spiteful, make life a misery, spoiling crops, souring milk. People learnt it was much better to stay on the good side of a Hob, than experience the bad. Come along now, ladies."

As we moved on, I knew we were all deliberately avoiding each other's eye. None of us quite knew what to make of our voluble guide. We didn't want to be rude, and the woman obviously had a wealth of knowledge when it came to local fables, folklore, and superstition, we just didn't know whether she was deliberately playing to the gallery, and we should laugh along with her, or whether she was as earnest as she seemed.

"Have you heard about the Gytrash?" she was asking now, "The inspiration behind the Hound of the Baskervilles, the terrifying black dog said to haunt the lonely Yorkshire roads, it even gets a mention in *Jane Eyre*. The Gytrash was known to lead travellers astray to their death and at night, even today, lone walkers hear him howling." A shiver ran down my spine, and I realised the further into the walk, and the deeper into the darkness of Steph's tales, the less inclined any of us were to laugh any more. Something else was adding to my unease. The more she talked, the more everything she was saying sounded familiar, there was a sense I'd heard them before, over and over, maybe as a child? Although I had no actual memory of exactly when.

There was no doubt we got our money's worth from our tour with Steph, but there was also no denying the lightening of our spirits as the tour ran its allotted time and Steph said goodbye, insisting on giving each of us a brief hug, and murmuring 'take care' in an unnervingly less than casual manner, before heading off. She looked back once at me and gave me a little nod of the head as if acknowledging something, God knows what, maybe we'd bonded over Mildred. I shuddered.

We made good use of our remaining days, seeing as much as we could of the North Yorkshire Coast and the moors. Lizzie and Sarah were taking turns at the driving with Alice riding shotgun. Nobody had actually said anything, but I guessed I'd been banned in case I blacked out, crashed, and killed us all – fair enough! At least it allowed me the benefit of simply sitting back to enjoy the amazing vivid purple of the heathers which thrived on the otherwise bleak moorland, giving it a unique appearance. And with the green, sheep-dotted fields, dry stone walls, and scattering of stone farm buildings, nobody was going to disagree. The scenery was sublime, we'd put any odd incidents from the last couple of days behind us, and I knew everyone was ten times more chilled than when we'd arrived. We didn't stint ourselves either, stopping for regular coffee, wine, and snack breaks, and took advantage of quaint little shops we discovered in villages, unashamedly stocking up on locally crafted scented candles, soaps and delicious chocolates.

One of our stops was picturesque Robin Hood's Bay, a smugglers' haven where steep stone steps took us down to the tiny harbour, laughing breathlessly at the fact that if we hadn't been fit when we arrived, we certainly would be by the time we left. It was with some relief that Lizzie, who was leading the way, pointed to the Bay Hotel. "Next stop, girls," she said, "Saw it in the guidebook, perfect place for a glass of chilled wine."

Seated with a view of the bay and the promised full glass, Sarah dipping into the crisps that had accompanied the drinks said idly, "Long way from Sherwood Forest." An old guy at the next table chuckled, "Sorry for butting in, ladies, but you don't know how many times we hear that – it's not that Robin, ours is an ancient forest spirit. I'm Steve, by the way. " He smiled, splitting his salt and pepper beard which matched his long hair, and the chocolate Labrador at his feet cocked its head as if confirming his point.

"Good God," exclaimed Alice, in mock horror, "You can't go two steps around here without tripping over another ghoul, goblin or ghastly story."

Steve's nod took her point, adding softly, "With such a magical place there is always more to discover." Looking up briefly, he caught my eye, and for just a few seconds his startlingly blue ones felt as though they saw right through to my soul, before he turned away again, ducking his head to his pint of Theakston's.

On our final day, we'd decided to drive over the moors – I think all of us wanted to make the most of the time we had left, and I certainly knew I wasn't thrilled at the thought of hopping back on the work treadmill. We lunched at a pub overlooking the River Esk and then in the shady picnic area settled down on Harris Tweed blankets packed by sensible Alice. Lying back and gazing at the sky I thought, "I'd really love to live here."

Alice snorted, "You of all people wouldn't last five minutes in the countryside!"

I wasn't even aware I'd voiced my thought aloud, but kept my voice light. "It's been amazing, all of us together, and I have rather fallen in love with the area."

Lizzie was surveying the list she'd put together for us. "We haven't had time to do the museum at Pannett Park, nor seen… " she paused dramatically then lowered her voice, drawing out the syllables, "...the Hand of Glory." The others laughed although my mind queasily went immediately to my dream and the black wizened fist grasping the dripping candle.

I think we were all tired, or maybe just too relaxed, because although there was more we could have done that afternoon, it was far more comfortable to just stay where we were until the sun started to set, and the chill in the air crept back. We quietly packed up to head back to the hotel. Sarah, our designated driver for this journey, decided on a different route back, although I think she might have regretted it because there were so many twists and turns, we held on to our stomachs! It was when we'd just rounded another sharp bend to see the road ascended a steep hill, that I saw the cottage. I started violently, and felt shock bring a chill to the base of my skull. Maybe I was mistaken, but no, it was the cottage from my dream. Sarah drove slowly to negotiate the combination of an S-bend before the road began to rise again. The cottage on my left side looked pretty derelict, even Hansel and Gretel might have turned their noses up, and then with an additional shock I saw it was for sale with the board of a local estate agent planted on the roadside. As I remembered to breathe again, I knew I couldn't say anything to the girls, but equally forcefully I knew I had to see inside with my own eyes. I made a mental note of the agent and phone number, thankful for my photographic memory, and I'd call as soon as we got back to the hotel.

The chatter of the others faded into the background as I rolled the craziness round my head, trying to make some kind of sense of it. There was no denying the ferocity and strength of my feelings but at the same time, no denying their lack of logic. I could recall the cottage so vividly from my dream, I knew exactly the configuration inside, I could hear Hettie saying things would start happening really quickly. Was this what she'd meant – but then it was just a dream, wasn't it? Even so I couldn't deny the sense I was coming alive here, all my senses on alert, my life in London like a faded and still fading photo in my mind. Lizzie asked me something, disturbing my reverie, and with an effort I forced myself back into the conversation.

What was left of our afternoon passed in a bit of a blur, and back at the hotel I was keying in the estate agent's number even as I opened the door to my room;

for a moment because it was late in the day, I was convinced they'd be closed, but my luck was in, and it sounded as if the woman on the other end felt much the same. She introduced herself as Charlotte, was delighted I was interested but with a frankness not always found, freely admitted the property was in a sorry state, empty for years. It needed total renovation, and unsurprisingly had been on their books for some time. She said she'd be happy to show me round – would 11.00 be good? I could tell from her tone she wasn't completely convinced by my enthusiasm; she'd probably been down that road with others before they were overwhelmed by the extent of the project. Logging into Rightmove, I realised I hadn't even asked Charlotte what it was on at, and was both pleased and worried to see just how low the price was. It was early 18th century, three bedrooms, and half an acre of garden backing onto a river and forest land.

Having a restless night's sleep, I tossed and turned for most of the night, not settling, my mind working in overdrive.

I hated keeping secrets from my friends, but if I couldn't explain the compulsion to myself, how could it possibly make sense to them, they'd think I'd gone totally crazy. I had a successful work life, designer home in an exclusive area of London, and a more than healthy bank balance. I was living the life dreamt of by many. Maybe I *was* totally crazy, the jury was still out.

CHAPTER 6

Our breakfast that morning was subdued. We always felt that way when we'd been together and then had to go our separate ways, although I had additional reasons on my mind. I felt dreadfully guilty, keeping such a major possible life change from them. Maybe I was wrong, they'd always supported me in every way. Feeling emotional, I had a sudden strong urge to cry, and made an excuse for a swift dash to the bathroom and a chance to pull myself together. The mirror showed a deathly pale reflection and I did some frantic cold water splashing before rummaging in my bag for some restorative makeup which did bring about a slight improvement.

Back at the table, nobody seemed to have noticed my mini meltdown, and Alice broke the silence. "You've been awesome, this has been the best hen party ever, I really feel I'm on the way to the big day now. And you, Lizzie, brilliant itinerary arranging, the festival, the ghost tour, we've crammed so much in, but we'll have to come back, there's still more to see."

"I'll upload all our pictures onto WhatsApp," I said, and Alice squeezed my arm, "Thanks, sweetie, can't wait to see them – and this hotel, ten out of ten for luxury!"

"Huh," put in Sarah, mock peeved, "Costumes?" Alice smiled. "I was getting to those – they were stunning, you know we couldn't have loved them more, and the work that went into them, was above and beyond." She paused. "I'm thrilled that you are making both my wedding dress, and the bridesmaids' dresses." Sarah made a face. "I've made an exception for you, I'm never going to be in the wedding market, all those bridezillas, they'd finish me off. Still one thing to be thankful for, none of us has to put up with those nipped-in waists, honestly the things women go through for fashion."

"You can say that again," I smiled round at them, "They certainly gave me a fit of the vapours, thank goodness we live now and not then."

"So," said Lizzie, "Agreed, we'll be back." I couldn't help thinking if my plan came to fruition they might be back sooner than they thought, but kept it to myself.

None of us are fans of big goodbyes, so quick hugs all round, promises to meet up again before the wedding, and then I was driving out of the hotel, relieved not to have given anything away of the turmoil I was in, and heading for Lavender Cottage, on what I reassured myself might simply be a flight of fancy that would come to nothing. After all, what I was considering would be a massive life-change. Was that what I really wanted?

I was still arguing with myself when I drove onto the pebbled drive at the side of the cottage about twenty minutes later. I was a little early and walked slowly up the garden path, waiting for Charlotte to arrive. It was so quiet here, the only sound birds calling in the trees and the murmur of the brook, almost obscured by overgrown ferns. There was no doubt the place needed a lot of TLC which I knew would equate to a fair bit of expense and that would be on top of the purchase, and then of course there'd be moving costs. I wasn't short of a penny or two, but did I really want this hassle? No, I resolved, I'd look inside, I didn't want the estate agent to feel I was messing her around, but I'd made up my mind, it was a hare-brained scheme, and I thanked my lucky stars I hadn't said anything to the others.

The flourishing, if untidy, bed of herbs from my dream was now overrun with waist-high weeds, while a bedraggled wisteria clung for dear life to the cottage's stone walls. I looked up to where a row of jackdaws were lined up on the roof, cawing because I was disturbing their peace. From this obviously popular roosting point their white droppings had liberally splashed the slated roof, and shielding my eyes with my hand I could see that further back a sapling was growing from the chimney stack, the putative tree looking a lot healthier than the chimney, which was tilting at a precarious angle; that would have to be seen to, although it could be the only thing holding the chimney on to the roof. I shook my head, wondering what was I thinking, this was only an exploratory visit. There was no way anyone, least of all me, would take on the headache of such a huge renovation project.

My thoughts were interrupted by Charlotte pulling up outside onto the drive, and exiting her Mini in a rush. My sort of age with blonde hair in an untidy high ponytail, she looked like someone not long out of bed after a heavy party the night before – I knew that feeling, although hoped I'd always been better at hiding it. Makeup looked as if it might have been applied in the car and her shirt was fast heading out of her skirt waistband.

"Ellie, so sorry, crisis in the office, couldn't get away, been waiting long?" Smiling, she held out her hand.

"No worries." I wasn't just being polite, and whereas normally I hated anyone turning up late, today I felt quite serene. "I've been taking in the garden. Looking forward to seeing inside." She glanced back at me curiously as she fiddled with the key in the lock, surprised perhaps that I'd waited instead of running a mile as previous viewers had done.

"The cottage has seen better days," she said, as she got the door open.

The understatement of the century, I thought.

"Are you looking for a holiday home?"

"Thinking of relocating, actually."

"You're in London, aren't you? I'd give my right arm to live there, not much to do around here, and as for night life," she pursed her lips, "Pretty non-existent." I didn't feel I needed to give her an explanation, especially as I didn't really have one, so contented myself with, "The grass is always greener, isn't it? And job pressures don't really give me much leisure time anyway. Life's work, work, work, falling into a bar most evenings, then starting over the next morning." Keen to change the subject, I said, "I imagine there's a history here?"

Charlotte slipped instantly back into estate agency mode. Apparently the cottage came under the ownership of the local landowner who'd recently passed away, but it hadn't been occupied for years, as was the case for most of his properties. His family hadn't felt inclined to take on such a major management and maintenance project, so were selling the whole portfolio, "But honestly, Ellie," she continued earnestly, "There are a good few more suitable properties closer to Whitby, new-builds, low maintenance, the Argyll Court development has amazing sea-view balconies, or you might prefer Whitehall Landing – spectacular views of the River Esk, and within walking distance of bars and restaurants."

I shook my head firmly, "No, I have that sort of property in London, looking for a change now and ..." She interrupted, "No problem, we have several older renovations if you're looking for peace and tranquillity, whereas this," she indicated to the now open cottage door, "Is a long-term doer-upper."

She was starting to get on my nerves. I didn't want to look at any other properties, so I might have been a little sharp. "I can't believe you're being so honest about the place, Charlotte. Almost feels as if you don't want to sell it, I'd have thought as it's been on Rightmove so long, you'd be biting my hand off." I paused as it occurred to me that maybe they preferred to sell it to a local, and she gave me a strange look, and I tried to lighten things up a bit. "In the past London agents have shown me round apartments that were more like broom cupboards, but they labelled them 'compact and bijou'."

"Well," she said, huffy not humorous, "I pride myself I can match a property to a person, and I don't think this is a fit for you. I pulled the short straw showing you around today." Seeing my expression, she must have realised how rude that sounded, because she drew close enough for me to smell a mint she must have popped in just before she arrived, maybe to mask last night's excesses. "This place has a reputation." I raised an eyebrow. "It's said that over 250 years ago this was home to a witch, they say she died a dreadful death, drowned in the river behind the cottage, morbid, right?"

I feigned shock, "No!" although this confirmed this was the place of my dream. "Still, you can't believe all these old wives' tales; all old properties have stories, don't they? But as we're here, it's a shame not to look."

In truth, I was pretty certain now that whatever state the cottage was in, it was going to be mine and she finally had no choice but to usher me in.

I recognised the room instantly despite the sorry state it was in. Cheap lino now covered the flagstones and two of the walls were painted dark green, while on the other two faded flowery wallpaper was peeling. There was a breeze coming through a broken window and in places plaster had crumbled to reveal the yellowish Yorkshire stone underneath. I would strip back some of the walls to expose the stone and I thought I might see if I could get the old range repaired.

In my memory the welcoming open fire crackled under the cooking pot giving off delicious smells, but coming back to the present the scent of damp and decay was overwhelming. Just then there was a rustling from the blacked fireplace and Charlotte jumped, shrieked and grabbed my arm, as a mouse ran across the room.

"As you can see," she murmured faintly, "Badly in need of modernisation." Although it was only late morning she was utilising the powerful torch she'd brought because it was dark inside the house. She was still holding my forearm, although I don't think she realised, and the house was definitely making her nervous, but all the things she saw as a problem didn't matter. To me, the house felt so right, I had a sense of belonging, of coming home. I tuned back in to a potted history,

"... last tenant was an old lady, think she lived here all her life, died some years ago – not here," Charlotte added hastily, "Hospital. Obviously, nothing's been done since, and I don't think it was brilliantly maintained even when she was here. It will need total rewiring, and plumbing – there's an old privy in the garden." She smiled at my expression, "Yes, an outside toilet, the older cottages around here still have them."

"Does that mean ..."

She nodded. "The old tin bath's still there – no indoor bathroom, I'm afraid." I could see this was the point at which she expected me to break and run.

"I see," I said mildly. "Well, you're right, there's obviously a great deal to be done, still it would give me a clean slate to make it totally my own, wouldn't it? What's in here?" We'd moved from the open kitchen/dining room into a much smaller room.

"Living room, I guess you'd call it," she said, "although given the size, probably more accurate to call it a snug, there's no room to swing a cat." I grinned inwardly; she really wasn't doing a great selling job.

"That's OK," I said, "I don't have one." She smiled uncertainly; she already had me down as a bit of a nutcase, wasn't entirely sure I was serious and apparently couldn't wait to finish off the viewing. There was no doubt about the faults she was pointing out, and looking round I saw I'd have to be inventive with this space, but on the positive side all the doors were massively solid, stripped pine, with the original heavy black wrought iron hinges and catches. There were signs of woodworm but I knew that could be treated, and the evidence of age only added to the charm of the place.

Upstairs, I followed Charlotte from room to room over carpeting which originally might have been green but was now too worn and stained to tell. Random pieces of furniture stood lonely and unconnected in the different rooms; an old, rusted metal bedframe stood below an ominous brown stained ceiling, which showed the roof needed attention, and a discarded upright chair, legs gnawed in places by goodness knows what, was set at an aimless angle in the middle of a room. Cast iron fireplaces in each bedroom were also rusted and in the corner of two of the rooms were mounds of shredded paper, on which I could see Charlotte was keeping a suspicious eye. One of the bedrooms was larger than the other two. "I could put a luxurious bathroom in here," I murmured almost to myself. Despite the appeal of authenticity, there was no way anyone was going to catch me outside in a tin bath, or using the privy. Charlotte nodded agreement. "A bathroom there would work if you didn't mind giving up the bedroom. On the plus side, the cottage is not listed so you shouldn't need planning permission for any internal renovations. But I must add, in the past the river has been known to burst its banks, although I don't believe any flooding got as far as the cottage." Then perhaps belatedly remembering her role, she added, "Look, Ellie, I've painted a bit of a doom and gloom picture, but on a positive note, I'm sure you'd get planning permission, if you wanted to extend the cottage"

I nodded absently; to me it was already a fairy-tale cottage, I was able to see past the decay and neglect, even the possibility of mice, rats, and any other wildlife the property might harbour didn't have me running for the hills. I knew I was going to buy the cottage and had the funds to do whatever was needed to make it what I wanted. I'd worked hard to build them up over years of hard slog and what better use to put them to? I'd need to find and commission a builder experienced in working with old properties, and maybe Hettie's hiding place would come to light.

Charlotte was getting impatient; she couldn't wait to leave, and was already ushering me towards the back door. "Let's just do a quick tour outside, shall we, Ellie?"

The garden was overgrown and would need work, but whilst I'm no Alan Titchmarsh, I could see beneath, and almost smothered by weeds and trailing ivy there were many mature bushes that I was sure could be brought back to the light of day. I could hear the sound of water running in the brook. She read my mind. "You've noticed the brook, it runs into the river." I nodded, "yes, it's magical."

"Beyond the river there are acres of forestland, certainly a secluded spot if that's what you want?" She didn't need to tell me this, I already knew. Neither of us was keen to explore the privy, but I'd keep it intact, it would make a perfect shed.

Completing our garden circuit brought us back to the front of the house.

"So, what do you think?" I could see Charlotte was starting to hope, against all the odds and logic, that she might possibly have a sale here.

"I'd like to offer the full asking price," I said. "I'm under no illusions, and I appreciate you've been honest and given me all the downsides, but I think with some TLC this could be just the place I'm after." She'd apparently psyched herself up for some serious price haggling, and her mouth dropped open. She instantly covered that by nodding enthusiastically.

"I have to sell my London place," I said, "But I can't see a problem, and I won't need a mortgage, I've got stacks of equity in the apartment." Charlotte nodded; her day was getting better and better, she was all smiles now, and she allowed her enthusiasm to get the better of her, giving me a quick hug.

"I can see you have wonderful plans and I'll look forward so much to seeing this place transformed. Let me just take some details and we can get the ball rolling."

CHAPTER 7

I was surprised when I got back to Richmond at just how low I felt, but it had been a long drive, and I always hated saying goodbye to the girls, so maybe that accounted for the sinking feeling as I swiped my card over the touch screen to access my apartment. I usually felt elated to get back to my luxury environment, but not this time. Things had changed. My dream apartment already felt part of my past. I didn't want to get back on the treadmill of work, hectic socialising, and more work, in fact there was a tight knot of anxiety in my stomach at the thought. My Yorkshire experiences seemed to have left me totally out of kilter. The sassy woman who left the apartment a week ago, was not the subdued one returning today from a time and world away.

There was no doubt in my mind when I got up the following morning, my opulent apartment had lost its lustre and that simply endorsed my decision. Even my view of the Thames, which normally lifted my spirits, did nothing for me today. My heart was back at the cottage, and I was impatient to get back too. I wanted to breathe crisp fresh air instead of London smog. My mind was working on overdrive, listing and planning things to be done and the order in which to do them. The sooner I kicked things into action, starting with my resignation letter, the less stressed I'd be. I'd called a local estate agent whilst I was still in the car outside the cottage, and arranged an appointment. I was, I'd told them, looking for a quick sale.

I'd picked an agent at random and hoped it was a good choice. When the buzzer sounded and I opened the door, I had my doubts. Was I really putting my future plans in the hands of a young man who looked as if he wasn't long out of school, or did he just look so young because I was getting older – a sobering thought? I must have glared at him because he nervously checked he had the right person and place. Dark slicked-back hair, pinstriped suit, flamboyant tie loosely knotted, and a whiter than white smile. He couldn't have looked more like an estate agent if he'd tried. I shook his offered hand firmly.

"Hi, Ellie, I'm Brett, I've come to give you a valuation." I had to bite my tongue, to avoid saying, 'Yes, as arranged'. "You're looking for a quick sale, I understand?"

"Absolutely. A quick sale is imperative."

He looked around. "Well, it's an awesome property! In one of the most sought after areas in West London, I see no reason why it shouldn't move quickly. Where are you looking to move to, perhaps we can help with your new property purchase?"

I really didn't want to explain or go into details. "Thank you, I have that all in hand."

"Where are you going?"

This was easier to answer. "Near Whitby."

"Whitby," he repeated, "Very nice, where's that then?" I was irritated. I didn't have high hopes of Brett and really didn't want to have another stab at conversation.

Moving over to the sofa I said, "I'll leave you to look around, then you can let me know what you think. Give me a shout when you've finished." Usually only this abrupt at work when I was under pressure, I caught the grimace on his face. Maybe I should soften up a bit, give the kid a chance to do his job.

When he'd measured and photographed, he found me in the kitchen. "Ellie, you have the most exquisite place, it wouldn't surprise me if we even get into a bidding war! A penthouse apartment with a Thames balcony view – extremely sought after. I think we're looking at two million, no question." He seemed a lot more confident now and had slipped into estate agent speak. I was pleased, it was more than I'd thought. That would give me a good healthy profit and plenty of funds for my move and the renovation work.

"As I said, I'm keen to get it on the market as soon as possible, and happy to sell it fully furnished, lock, stock and barrel. Nothing here will fit into my new place." He gave me a doubtful look.

"You sure? You must have spent a fortune kitting this place out?"

"Absolutely."

He smiled, "OK, well that makes things even easier. Right, that's me done. I have the contract here for you to read, and sign if you're happy with everything?" He passed me the paperwork and a pen. After a quick check and a bit of speed reading, I was satisfied, and signed, dated, then passed the form back to him. I didn't even worry about negotiating a better deal on the commission – I didn't want any delays. He stacked the papers. "Thank you, I have a list of clients on my books looking for properties like this. I'll hit the phones as soon as I get back." I was feeling guilty I'd been so judgemental. I smiled and thanked him, and he smiled back, far more relaxed now he'd closed at least one end of the deal. He assured me he'd keep me up to date at every stage and I was glad to show him the door.

Well, I'd just made one of the most momentous decisions of my life. I poured myself a large glass of chilled wine, a little early in the day, but some nerves needed calming, and it's always wine o'clock somewhere in the world! It was such a dramatic change, and made in such a short space of time, there was bound to be some major emotional fallout, especially when I told my parents and friends. There were things I couldn't share with them, the dreams, the crazy experience in Whitby, and the true reason for the move. I'd have to have a pretty cast-iron story in the background, but I shrugged this off. I'd deal with everything one step at a time.

First on the action list was to hand in my resignation at work on Monday morning. Next, I'd call my parents. I'd arrange a weekend with them. I wasn't going to tell them over the phone. I didn't expect them to understand that their talented, high-flying daughter planned to throw everything away on a whim, and knew they'd do everything possible to persuade me to change my mind, which was why I planned to hand my notice in first.

I was also dying to tell Alice, Sarah, and Lizzie, but had decided I'd wait until after Alice and Robbie's wedding and honeymoon. I didn't want to take attention away from their big day. But of course I'd have to give them a sanitized version of what was going on sometime soon, they knew me too well. The girls wouldn't pull their punches, saying exactly what they thought of my crazy scheme, swapping my luxury lifestyle, dazzling career, and stunning Thames-side penthouse for a cottage with a tin bath, an outside toilet, and no plan of what I was going to do moving forward. I'd put Hettie to the back of my mind, and what with everything going on, she resurfaced now as a welcome friend in these times of turmoil.

I'd asked Mike to pick me up a little earlier than usual on Monday morning, and I had my resignation letter safely stored in my Mulberry bag. I had an overwhelming feeling of relief having made my decision. I chose an extra strong double espresso from the coffee shop, feeling a kick of energy would do me no harm and might provide some fortitude, I was nervous about the reaction of my boss. Wanting to get the confrontation out of the way as soon as possible, I headed straight to his office. He must have guessed something was up, because he was already frowning. "Ellie, good to see you back, pleasant week?"

"Brilliant, thanks, can I have a quick word?"

"What can I do for you?" I knew I was seen as one

of the low-maintenance advertising executives, and rarely needed time with Simon other than running through my quarterly reviews and bonus statements. It was well known that once clients were working with me, they stayed. I passed the letter over straight away; Simon raised an eyebrow then took his time opening and reading it. When he'd finished he looked genuinely shell-shocked. "Whoa," he said, "I didn't see this coming, I really didn't, especially from you."

It was difficult to look him in the eye, so I was carefully scrutinising my hands. "I didn't either, Simon, it's just while I was in Yorkshire I had a moment of clarity, and everything changed for me. I just feel this is something I have to do."

There was a brief silence then he said, "Any point in trying to change your mind?" I shook my head. "Thought not." He cleared his throat, "Well it's a real shame, particularly as while you were away a new client asked especially to work with you." He paused. "It's a biggie, and right up your street!" I didn't say anything, and he sighed, "Looks like I'll have to deal with her myself then."

Curiosity got the better of me. "OK, I'll bite, who is it?"

He shook his head. "Now, now, you really don't expect me to say, do you? Especially as she was all a bit cloak and dagger anyway!"

I grinned in acknowledgement. "You don't have to worry, I won't go after her on my own, I'm done with the advertising business."

He shrugged. "Force of habit, can't be too careful. As a matter of fact she was pretty vague, but insisted it was you she wanted, said a woman would be on the right wavelength. She knew a lot about your past campaigns, gave us to understand she was looking for something right at the top end, both budget and creative-wise." He frowned momentarily. "Eccentric character, not quite what you'd expect. I didn't actually talk to her for long, she saw Oli, he just brought her in to introduce us." He shook his head, recalling. "Dressed up as if off to a fancy dress party, or a Victorian music hall," he sniggered, "Maybe she was headed to one of those themed parties every corporate's doing nowadays. Anyway, seemed nice enough." He raised an eyebrow at me again. "Intrigued?"

I laughed, "Not taking the bait, Simon." But the laugh was hollow and my voice a little shaky. I'd begun to feel oddly uncomfortable, the feeling at first barely noticeable but then building, chilling, giving me that 'goose walked over my grave' shiver. Maybe I'd been more apprehensive about telling Simon than I'd thought and it was catching up with me now.

He misinterpreted my expression. "Don't look so worried, if your mind's made up, it's made up, I'm not going to put any more pressure on, I know you, once you make a decision you don't budge."

He leaned back in his chair and the atmosphere changed from personal to businesslike. "Right, well you know you're contractually obliged to give three months' notice from today but I have to put you on immediate garden leave. This means today's your last day in the office, I'll call HR and they'll run through the full leaving process."

"Understood," I said, now feeling surprisingly calm.

Lightening his tone he added, "Obviously we'll arrange a cracking leaving do for you, and I'll make sure everyone knows about this." He added as one last try, "As long as you really are sure?"

"I am, I've already put my apartment on the market, I'm moving to the North Yorkshire Moors" He came round the desk to hug me. As he was usually undemonstrative, the gesture caught me by surprise, and I think it did him as well. "You've been one of the best execs I've worked with. And you know we all love you. You'll stay in touch, and drop in to see us, won't you?"

"I will, of course I will" I assured him although I knew I wasn't planning on coming back to London any time soon, so my words were shallow, his too probably.

When Simon called for everyone's attention in the board room a short time later, people were still catching up from the weekend, making themselves a coffee or helping themselves to water from the dispenser. They looked worried; there had been rumours of redundancies. But as they all settled at the table he immediately said, "I have to tell you Ellie handed in her notice this morning, she's moving to the countryside, the North Yorkshire Moors to be precise! Obviously, I'm devastated, as you can imagine, she's been one of the best. But more than that she's a fab person, she'll be truly missed." I had my eyes on my notebook and heard mutterings of, "Jeez, what the hell?" and, "Oh my God." And I studiously didn't look up.

Simon continued, "I know this is a shock for everyone, but I'm sure we wish Ellie well, she's been one in a million." And then he moved swiftly on to the rest of the meeting. Strange, such a major decision yet here it was made, announced, and actioned, no turning back now.

When the meeting ended, I was bombarded. The general thinking seemed to be it was a crazy decision, I'd worked so hard to get where I was, and a couple of them said they were prepared to lay money on the fact I'd be back before too long. Mind you, I think there were also one or two who were hiding their pleasure at the prospect of less competition in the workplace!

Once we were all back at our desks, Oli, one of my best friends, trotted over to envelop me in his arms. We'd started at the agency at the same time and clicked from the start. He was a flamboyant character and always overreacted, or as he sometimes said with a laugh, 'overacted!'

"OMG, Ellie, what are you doing?" Now he was sounding genuinely horrified. "I know you've put the brakes on the party lifestyle, but no-one expected this. This isn't some kind of wind-up, is it?" He held me at arm's length, scrutinising my face, ready for me to say "Gotcha!" but I shook my head slowly. "I know you think I'm crazy, but this is the best thing for me, right now. Only thing I'm going to miss is your ugly mug, cheering me up every day. You will come and visit, won't you?"

He twisted his mobile features to show shock. "What, in the countryside? Me, in wellies wading through mud? Darling, I think not." Then seeing my face fall, "Oh don't look like that, of course I will, silly girl." He gave me his wide grin. "In the meantime, I shall dive headlong into devising the send-off of all send-offs for you, and you'll be so stricken with guilt you'll have to change your mind."

"You're a star, thank you, but I honestly don't want too much of a fuss."

"You just leave it to your Uncle Oli," he said, which reassured me not one jot. "By the way, who's the new client, Simon wouldn't spill the beans?" He laughed, "Oh darling, some woman named Em Corey. I did a bit of my own research, turns out she owns a humungous cosmetics company called Tuttuba, with her partners, Good and Nurse. They're based somewhere near Boston, in the US, have you heard of them?" I shook my head. "She looked more like a member of a grunge band though!" Before I could answer we spotted Simon frowning at us, and Oli did an exaggerated pantomime tip-toe back to his own desk, to laughter from the rest of the office.

I had surprisingly little personal stuff to take home, and what I did have fitted easily into my Mulberry bag. All around me my colleagues – ex colleagues – were working and I had to suppress the smile that kept creeping onto my face; this all felt so right. I didn't even wait for 5.30 to call Mike for the last time to take me home.

CHAPTER 8

In the weeks following my resignation, work had become almost a distant memory, and there was no doubt I was already enjoying my less complicated life. I was getting used to spending time on my own, and enjoying the company. I couldn't remember when I'd last had so much time on my hands. For the last few years my life had revolved around work, socialising, and obsessively keeping fit. In retrospect it seemed a shallow existence, and with its going I felt the weight of the world had been lifted from my shoulders. I cancelled my gym membership, and all but the most essential beauty appointments, I wasn't out to impress anymore. Most of my time was spent out of doors, whatever the weather, and even the rain didn't deter me, it meant fewer people around. I'd pull on my sports gear, baseball cap, wraparound shades, and walk the towpath alongside the Thames or enjoy a run through Richmond Park, smiling at the fallow deer roaming freely.

Conscious that my remaining time in London was limited, I acted the tourist, and crammed in as many museums and art galleries as I could. I must confess I was a little surprised, annoyed even, that with all that fresh air and exercise, my hair still felt brittle, and despite doing double duty with the moisturiser my skin was dry, my usual olive glow grown sallow. Maybe the girls had a point, time to see a specialist?

I realised I hadn't been dreaming of Hettie during the past weeks; maybe she had nothing to tell me, maybe she knew I was getting on with things as planned. I realised I'd become almost reclusive, I'd cut down on social media and no longer obsessively waited for messages; what a relief not to be checking every few seconds. Nowadays I kept my mobile on silent, and in fact there were very few messages, certainly none from work colleagues despite their gushing farewells. The only exception was Oli. He was a keeper, and I knew we'd always stay in touch. He played camply flamboyant and sarcastic, but beneath that was a caring heart and a listening ear. Next on the list was to tell my parents, and friends. I'd call my parents after the wedding and hopefully arrange to see them the weekend after if they were free. They were usually so busy with their own social engagements, but I'd feel infinitely relieved once I'd shared my news with them. Alice's wedding was coming up and I'd decided my news would keep until after the celebrations. I wanted Alice and Robbie to have their fairy-tale wedding without any undue stress, and truth be told I couldn't imagine for one moment what my friends would make of my plans, and I knew when I did tell them they wouldn't hold back.

Talking, planning and WhatsApping about the wedding seemed to have gone on for ever, and now the day before had finally arrived. I was beside myself with excitement. Weddings aren't normally my bag, but this was Alice, so it couldn't be more special. I was flying up to Edinburgh on the Friday and making my way home again on the Sunday afternoon. Sarah had taken measurements for our bridesmaid dresses ages ago, and we were meeting at our hotel chosen for its proximity to the wedding venue. We'd be able to try on our dresses then, and Sarah was bringing an emergency kit with her, should any disasters arise, or tweaks be needed. She was always the calmest of us all, but I could see from her messages, at the moment she was under a lot of pressure – she had big responsibilities.

I'd originally planned to travel with just a carry-on case, but as so often happens realised that just wasn't going to do the trick. I'd cut down drastically, but still needed skin-care products, makeup, wedding shoes – natural silk thankfully and fitting like a glove – as well as a change of dress for the dancing. Once checked into my lush hotel room, I had a message from Lizzie, she was already here. A short time later once I'd freshened up, we both headed to Sarah's room for the trying-on session. All the dresses had been couriered to the hotel a couple of days previously, and looked awesome but I know we were all a little nerve-wracked in case they didn't fit. I should have had more faith. Sarah might be a bit scatty and invariably late for most things, but she'd never let us down yet.

Alice and Sarah had kept the design of the bridesmaids' dresses to themselves – ignoring our original demands to choose our own dresses – but we needn't have worried, Lizzie and I donned gorgeously understated glamorous gowns. For her bridal dress Alice had opted for an elegantly simple look with a long sheath-like design, in a natural tone. The material felt divine, cleverly accentuating our individual body shapes. Delighted, we struck poses in front of the full length mirror and Sarah sank down on the bed for a moment. "Oh, thank God! And well done for not losing or putting on any weight, you do know I'd have had to kill you, don't you? Now look," she said as she passed us a rectangular box each. "A special gift to wear with the dress." The delicate pearl necklace, matching earrings, and bracelet were gorgeous and nearly finished me off. I swallowed hard and could see Lizzie struggling too. "Come on now, save that for tomorrow," Sarah said briskly, and continued, "Bouquets are white tulips – Alice saw this style in a magazine and fell in love, apparently they're popular in the Netherlands." Lizzie nodded. "I've seen it too. Has Alice tried on her dress yet?"

"Last night," confirmed Sarah, "We did it straight away, and all is well. Lizzie, for goodness sake, what's the matter now?" Lizzie had taken Sarah's place on the edge of the bed and was in full flow. "Take no notice," she said, reaching for a tissue, and blowing her nose in a most un-bridesmaid-like way. "It's just it's all so lovely." Sarah laughed, but we could see she was a bit wobbly too. "OK," she said, reverting to the practical. "Let's get both of you out of the dresses before you slobber all over them." She suited action to word and in no time the precious dresses were back in their protective zip-up bags, and we had a good laugh at just how emotional we were all feeling, had a comforting hug and agreed to meet at the bar later for a calming glass of chilled wine.

On the morning of the wedding our taxi arrived promptly to convey us to the Signet library, our route taking us along the Royal Mile, and craning out the window we agreed there could be no better spot for our next group get-together, loads of tempting shops and some great looking places to eat. We were certain we'd hear no objections from Alice when we got around to mooting the idea.

Making our way through the impressive wrought iron gates into the expansive Georgian reception hall, we agreed Alice and Robbie couldn't have picked a better venue for the occasion. We stopped briefly at the foot of the sweeping, incredibly impressive mahogany staircase to watch the piper setting up in the hall and practising the lament – the otherworldly wailing bouncing back from the surrounding wooden panelling. The tall bearskin hat he'd don later was by his side, and he was pretty impressive himself, kilted and sporran-ed with a bright red sash, the regalia finished to perfection by tartan-trimmed long black and white boots. Aware of us watching, he turned and gave us a wink before returning, ruddy cheeked, to the not so easy task of working the pipes.

The Signet library was to our right, and was a hive of activity, plush red velvet chairs being carefully set out for the ceremony, and the string quartet setting up near the wide Georgian window. They were good friends of the happy couple, so the music would be all the more special. I was idly wondering what they'd chosen to play, when a tall, broadly built woman accosted us, height and build exaggerated by black patents with sky high heels, and a figure-hugging deep red bandage dress. I didn't need to look at the others to know they were also thinking that going up a size on the dress might have made for a better look.

"Stacey, wedding planner," she announced, "Glad you're early, thought I might have to chase you up. Are those guys," she indicated with her chin, "ushers and best man?" We shrugged, we were as much in the dark as she appeared to be. Stacey took action and was soon striding back with the group trailing obediently behind. I could see she was a woman it wouldn't be easy to say no to. In different coloured tartan kilts – I wondered briefly if these were genuine 'clan colours' or simply what the hire shop had to hand – black shirts, jackets and tartan ties matching each kilt, the guys looked good. One of them looked remarkably like Robbie, obviously brother, possibly a twin? Sarah and Lizzie, both of whom were single at the moment, didn't look displeased at these additions to the party. I was single too, but right now my focus was on life changes rather than relationships – the last thing I needed was complications.

Robbie's brother did indeed turn out to be his twin, he introduced himself as Ali and gave us a familiar 'Robbie' smile. Stacey swung round and frowned at the interruption; she was issuing instructions and obviously felt he wasn't paying the attention he should be. I hadn't taken to the woman but could sympathise with just how difficult a task wedding planners took on, not only having to ensure the smooth running of the event but dealing with brides in varying stages of panic. I love Alice to bits but knew how impatient and demanding she could be. The dresses and floral arrangements were all designed to look natural, casually put together at the last minute, but I knew there was nothing more carefully planned than this type of 'natural', and that Alice would have researched everything to the nth degree.

"Pay attention." Stacey clapped her hands to command our concentration, and I exchanged an amused look with Ali. In my head I'd nicknamed Stacey the Staffordshire bull terrier, but actually what did it matter as long as she got everything perfect for Alice. "Right," she continued, we're going to do a quick tour, show you the facilities, I'll run through the order of service, and go through your duties." Duties? I might have sniggered softly because she gave me a cold stare, not noticing Sarah who gave us a goofy look, making Lizzie and me turn away quickly before we showed ourselves up further. We both knew once we started, stopping wouldn't be an option. It was always the case that the more inappropriate the situation, the more uncontrollable the laughter, like when I'd giggled my way through the funeral service of one of our university professors.

"Here." She waved her arm indicating the room in which we were standing. "Is where the guests will assemble after the ceremony. Now, follow me." And we trailed dutifully in her wake as she whisked us through the elegant Georgian library with its antique books, lots of mahogany, massively potted palms and several chandeliers. All very grand. Stacey held up a hand to halt us, and bullet-pointed: "Pre-wedding canapés and champagne. Guests directed here once ushers have handed them order of service. Bride's family and friends to the left. Bridegroom's to the right. First front rows close family only – got it?" The ushers chorused assent, and didn't seem particularly bothered that she was talking to them as if they were five years old. Maybe just the Scottish way? "It's not a religious service." Stacey paused and sniffed, leaving no doubt of her views on that, before continuing, "A celebrant will take the service. You'll find all the details of music etc in the order of service, see, over there, the box by the stairs. Now," she barked. "Best man!" Ali stepped forward, raising his hand in unconscious confirmation of the teacher/school child dynamic. "OK, you'll wait for the groom in reception then bring him down the aisle to the floral archway over there, got that?" Ali solemnly confirmed he had.

"Bridesmaids? I want you in the reception area until bride arrives, and I do not want you disappearing into the loo just at the point you're needed. Understand?" We nodded. "You follow the bride, as she makes her way to meet her groom." We nodded again, giggling in check, and she frowned for a moment, unsure whether we were taking this seriously enough. "I will cue the string quartet, when you're ready for the off." Zoning out, I wondered what song Alice had chosen as I watched the florists putting final touches to the archway where Alice and Robbie would tie the knot. More flowers were being threaded through the ends of seating rows and the scent was almost overpowering.

Stacey broke my reverie. "Come along now, chop, chop. Just enough time for the quick tour," she declared, "So you know where everything else is, in case people want directions." Trotting up the sweeping mahogany staircase, we couldn't help but admire the beautifully painted and ornate domed ceiling. Women draped in Grecian style dusky pink gowns were interspersed with chubby cherubs on clouds. The magnificent room Stacey led us into had marble effect baroque columns, ornate gold finials, and a mock Roman feel. Pristine white-clothed tables bore elegantly tall flower arrangements around candles ready to be lit. "Bathrooms." Stacy waved a hand as we whisked past marked doors and added, "I trust as supporters of the happy couple, you will limit alcohol consumption." In our group nobody exchanged looks but I knew we were all thinking the same, and would probably not be following Stacy's orders.

Downstairs again, the quartet were practising 'Beautiful' by Christina Aguilera. The piper was taking up position in the hallway ready to welcome in the first guests, and from then on, it was all systems go!

Guests all gathered in the library, the room buzzed with conversation, champagne glasses clinked and canapés were being eagerly consumed amid cries of delight from those who hadn't seen each other for ages. We were still waiting patiently for Alice to pitch up, and my stomach rumbled as I caught glimpses of the delicacies doing the rounds but I wasn't going to risk the wrath of Stacey if I was caught with a mouthful of smoked salmon at a crucial moment. Robbie had arrived to be greeted with an emotional hug by Ali, and led into the library where spontaneous clapping broke out. And then, at an audible gasp from Lizzie, I turned to see Alice and her father making their way into the hallway.

Alice was a vision of understated elegance, with the delicate dress accentuating her petite figure. She looked sublime, and as Sarah helped straighten her dress, they exchanged huge smiles and Alice softly whispered, "thank you!" Stacey was waiting by the library door, raised her eyebrows in a clear 'are you ready?' way then turned and cued the quartet, and we slowly followed Alice and her father down the aisle to the strains of 'A Thousand Years', one of my favourites! A real tear-jerker at the best of times. I immediately felt myself welling up, and didn't dare look at the others as we moved closer to Robbie waiting under the floral archway, and the guests on either side of the flower-scented aisle started clapping; at first softly as Alice passed, then louder and louder, and we followed our captivating friend towards the next chapter in her life.

It was the best wedding ever and left me feeling as if I was walking on air. As we made a quick detour to the Ladies', after the ceremony, Sarah gave a tremulous sigh. "Now at least I can relax, and have some fun! Honestly, girls, I can't tell you how sick I've been feeling ever since I got up, but thank goodness all's well. Now I intend to let my hair down, and party!" We grinned, no argument from us. We were seated next to the top table with the ushers, and canny Alice, attempting to match-make like all happy brides, had mixed us all up. I wasn't looking for romance but was hugely relieved that this arrangement meant I wasn't going to be pushed into any deep and meaningful conversations with my friends.

Sitting between Cameron and James, it turned out they'd both known Robbie since schooldays. James was full of nervous energy – perhaps a good match for Lizzie, I thought.

"Do you still live in Scotland?" I asked.

He smiled, shook his head. "Despite the accent, I moved away years ago. Live in the North Yorkshire Moors, a village around twenty miles inland."

"Alice's hen do was in Whitby," I said, "We had a blast."

He grinned. "Aye, I heard. But to be honest I steer clear these days, it's always overrun with tourists. When I go to the coast it's usually Runswick, or Robin Hood's Bay."

"We went there," I said, "loved the area, specially the spooky folk stories."

"Funny you should say that." James lowered his voice. "There've been some funny rumours lately of witches returning to the Whitby area, mind you," he paused for dramatic effect, "There's some say maybe they never left! There've been strange occurrences over the years."

I was uneasy now, but played along. "Well, we certainly saw ghosts, ghouls, and vampires by the dozen – but no, can't say I recall any witches."

James smiled and shook his head. "I know, I know, the Goth thing – I did that once before, quite an experience. But I don't mean that, I can see you don't believe me, and I know some of the locals are way too superstitious, but there are some things nobody can explain."

"Oh give over," I said, "Maybe Yorkshire men are just intimidated by strong females, isn't it proven witches were just wise women?" I wasn't usually one for banging the feminist drum, I always imagined them with hairy armpits and a lack of personal hygiene, but I was intrigued by the rumours. "So," I challenged him, "If it's true, let's hear more about these rumours, where are they coming from?"

He gave me a theatrical wink. "Couldn't tell you my sources, now could I?" And at that point his attention was caught by the girl on his other side asking was there any more of the white wine? I'd lost him and I could see by the way he was steadily knocking back the drink, I'd probably get no more sense out of him than I had already.

With the authoritative clinking of spoon on glass, best man Ali was calling for our attention. "Ladies and gentlemen, can we all rise to toast the gorgeous bride and her dashing groom, Alice and Robbie," and then we were right into toasts and speeches and more toasts and indeed yes, more speeches.

I have to confess it was a bit of a relief when all the clapping and toasting came to a halt, and I could turn to my right to chat to Cameron. I was glad he'd kept his alcoholic intake to a more sensible level. He was a broker, based in Edinburgh and I knew enough about the business from friends to be able to chat intelligently enough, and when he asked what I did, I told him and didn't mention I'd actually given up my job, didn't want Lizzie or Sarah overhearing. Although it was easy to talk about a world I knew, at the back of my mind were James's cryptic comments, and I was frustrated not to have gained more information about whatever was supposed to be going on in Whitby.

Whilst the tables were being cleared and moved, we dashed up to our allocated room to change into more comfortable dresses for dancing and re-entered the transformed room, as the traditional Ceilidh band played, launching the Scottish dancing. Cameron grabbed me by the hand and dragged me onto the dance floor, and I let myself go. As we swirled around the room, kilts and gowns twirling, I cheekily wondered, would I find out what was under a Scotsman's kilt! Toes trodden on left, right and centre, but who cared when everyone was letting their hair down. The steps might not have been perfect, but that was fine too. Like performers in a badly directed period drama, we danced at breakneck speed, caution cast to the wind in the pleasure of music and movement.

As I continued to spin, I spotted James, arms crossed firmly on his chest, had nodded off on a chair in the corner of the room, so we were unlikely to have a rerun of our earlier conversation. There were in fact quite a number of people around the room who had 'checked out' early, having peaked too soon. Luckily the girls and I were usually expert at striking just the right balance, knew our limits, and when to start topping up our glasses with water. I did though have to admit on this occasion I might not have been quite so scrupulous, but the atmosphere was riotous, the dancing intense, the champagne flowing, and the occasion couldn't have been happier. I don't think we set our bottoms on a seat until early evening when a traditional afternoon tea was served, which gave us a much needed rest and energy boost, and then we hit the dancefloor again with Alice who was radiating happiness as we strutted our stuff to the Spice Girls Tribute Band. The four of us danced and sang until we could sing no more!

When we got back to our hotel, well after midnight, I barely made it to the room before kicking off my shoes. Earlier they'd been so comfortable, now they felt like instruments of torture. I was certain I was covered in bruises from the boisterous dancing, and my voice was now more of a croak. I still had on my dress but honestly didn't have the energy to do anything about it, and abandoning my usual strict routine of makeup removal and moisturising, flopped down on the bed. The room was spinning so I shut my eyes although then I was spinning. And suddenly I was back inside the cottage – my cottage, but Hettie's time.

She was standing on the other side of the room, and even in this oddest of situations something didn't feel right, something was off kilter. I realised it was because I seemed to have one foot in one time zone, and the other in the not so distant past. Before me was the old hearth, the fire lit, and the cooking pot steaming, yet the floor was covered in the tatty lino I'd seen when I was last there with the reluctant estate agent, and there was electric lighting around the room, no candles, no Hand of Glory in sight. Hettie's mouth was moving, but try as I might, I could barely hear her. Like a badly tuned radio she kept going in and out of earshot, every other word inaudible. She was distressed, gesticulating wildly, pointing frantically at the window, desperately trying to tell me something, but I just couldn't hear. Then the lights began flashing on and off, making the scene dizzily disorientating as if we were in a horror movie. Rooted to the spot, I couldn't get any nearer to Hettie and she was fading in and out visually now as well, zoning in and out in time with the lights. The atmosphere felt increasingly menacing. I knew someone was outside in the garden, outside but looking in. I couldn't see who, but I felt malevolence and my skin goose-pimpled. Suddenly the room was plunged into total pitch black darkness, the fire extinguished. Then I was enveloped in a strong, freezing wind, lifting and twisting me before I fell to the floor, and a child's voice, sweet and high rose in song, "ring a ring o' roses, a pocket full of posies, atishoo, atishoo, we all fall down."

I felt frozen to the bone, as an overwhelmingly familiar stench surged into my nose and mouth, rotten eggs, sourly clogged drains and urine, the same foul aroma that had overwhelmed me in Whitby. Involuntarily I gagged, then gagged again, and then I was on the floor, on carpet, my evening gown tangled around my legs and there was just one urgency – reaching the bathroom. With seconds to spare, I violently voided the contents of my stomach into the toilet bowl. I waited a while to see what else might be forthcoming, but it appeared I'd rid myself of the problem in one fell swoop. My abdomen felt as if I'd been kicked by a donkey, I had a bone-dry mouth and a head that was redefining the word throbbing. I made it back to my suitcase, and scrabbled around to locate a couple of Paracetamol; why is it you can never get the damn things out of the foil when you need them in a hurry? I glugged down the pills, and held my aching head in my hands. In confusion and in vain I struggled to remember the disturbing dream from last night. In the pale cold light of creeping dawn it seemed just out of reach and yet a whole world away.

As I straightened I caught an accidental glimpse of myself in the mirror, and jerked reflexively, as a horror story gazed back. Mascara and eye liner mingled and ran down my cheeks, my lipstick had faded and smudged, giving me a clown-like appearance. I'd had a spray tan before the wedding, but now it merely made me look grubby. The bedding on the floor was smeared with makeup and tan, there was bound to be a surcharge to pay, but worse than that, it looked so sleazy. I was mortified and angry at myself.

Pulling myself together a little, and reasoning a shower would only complicate the spray tan situation, I stripped off and gingerly washed with face wipes. Generously applying concealer and foundation to my face made some improvement, and I cleaned my teeth twice, rinsing with mouthwash so at least my breath felt fresher and hopefully wouldn't knock anyone out. I dressed in a simple pair of trousers, shirt, blazer and loafers, ready for the journey home, starting to feel a little more human. I wasn't hungry but I was gasping for a coffee. I didn't think I could be bothered with the instant in the room, I needed something altogether stronger. I'd head down for breakfast earlier than planned, and at least the waves of nausea were slowly fading. Maybe a couple of slices of dry toast would do me good? Pulling the tangle teaser through my unruly locks, I tied it in a high ponytail, spraying it liberally with hairspray to tame it a little.

I was sorely troubled. I knew Hettie had been in the dream; was it a dream? And was certain she'd been trying to tell me something crucial. But the more I tried to recall, the less I could remember, I knew I'd missed something significant, probably way too much champagne had impaired my memory. I just hoped I'd get another chance – *I'm so sorry, Hettie, I know you needed to tell me something, I let you down.*

CHAPTER 9

The following weekend, on a leisurely drive down to my childhood home in Surrey, I had a fair amount of time for reflection. Sandy, my mother, hadn't ever approved of Mummy, Mother, or Mum, and my father had followed suit, so I always called them by name. At school none of my friends thought this was in any way odd, in fact they decided my parents were dead cool. This couldn't have been further from the truth; my mother ruled the roost with an iron rod, softened only by a saccharine and insincere smile, and Geoff, my father, went along with that most of the time, anything for an easy life. But she did like to be liked and gave a deliberately more laid back impression when my friends, or indeed anybody else, came over. She was a great one for palling up with my friends' mothers and flirting outrageously with their fathers.

My parents had their own love story, their own secret language that excluded me. I was the cuckoo in the nest, always feeling like an interloper. There was emotional distance between us but that didn't prevent their sky-high expectations of me, and despite my best efforts I always felt I fell short. They made me feel as if I was a project they'd undertaken that hadn't quite worked out as planned. Even now, having achieved financial success, seen by everyone else as a high-flier, I still walked away each time I saw my parents feeling deflated. Over the years I'd probably read every self-help book going, had analysed till I ached but was probably none the wiser now as an adult than I was during all my growing-up years. On a positive note it had certainly made me a self-sufficient, driven individual, albeit one with major commitment and emotional issues.

I was feeling far more settled in the peaceful new life I'd adopted and was beyond relieved that this was my new normal, but I had an uneasy feeling in my bones that my drive down was simply the calm before the storm. There was no way my parents were going to take my news well and I knew we were set for some awkward conversations.

Despite their high aspirations for me, my parents certainly didn't come from gilded backgrounds themselves, they'd worked their own way up to the lifestyle they enjoyed today. My mother had always fended for herself, living with her alcoholic, unemployed mother in a high-rise flat in one of London's less salubrious areas. She lacked both love and material support and realised the only way to drag herself up was going to be successfully climbing the educational ladder. Passing her 11 Plus, and getting into an exclusive grammar school was her first step, although her mother could barely scrape together enough for the uniform, let alone the books required. With a stroke of luck a kind teacher had helped, ensuring she was supplied with study material, and a second-hand uniform.

Over the years my mother and I, as hot headed and stubborn as each other, had got into some spectacular arguments. My father, who played the passive role in our family dynamic, tended on such occasions to remember something desperately urgent that needed doing somewhere else, and left us to it. Harking back to her own childhood was a constant, and she'd get so angry if I fell short of what she expected. One particular argument lingered longer in my mind than others. I was about fourteen, a difficult age, and I can't even remember what set her off, I suppose I must have said something, and she blew up.

"You ungrateful little madam, you don't know how good you've got it. I had to wash all my own clothes from the age of six, everyone teased me about my hair – which I had to cut myself – and everyone else, every single person came to school with a crisp white hanky every day while I had a scrunched up piece of toilet tissue shoved up my sleeve!"

Moments like this scared me, what was clear was the shame and raw anger that lingered alongside bitter memories that were still with her today. I understood she was taking her feelings out on, but not really at, me. I knew she had few friends at school. They called her "fleabag", she never looked particularly clean in her second-hand clothes, and it was common knowledge she had free school dinners.

I gathered at playtime she'd wander around the noisy playground with plenty of time to stretch her imagination, invent her own stories. She was an avid reader because it was something you could comfortably do on your own, and at the same time she told herself she was glad to be expanding her knowledge. Possibly these days she wouldn't have fallen through the social services cracks, might even have been taken into care. I sympathised, of course I did, but it was hard to empathise, she was right when she said it was so far removed from all my own experiences.

She'd been forced to become the mistress of reinvention and her success in that was partly due to her sewing machine. It was an infinitely precious possession, carefully hidden from her mother who, if she ever laid hands on it, would sell it without a second thought. The machine only emerged when her mother had passed out from another drinking session. My mother had a natural talent and became more and more skilled as time went on and she designed and made all her own clothes. She even got a part time job with Biba, the ultimate cool in fashion stores. There was no question about them taking her on, they immediately fell for her effortlessly unique and stylish look, and she was an excellent saleswoman. By the time she started university, no-one could have guessed her background. The ugly duckling, purely due to her own hard paddling, had matured into a rather impressive swan.

She'd gained a full scholarship to Oxford and turned her back on her own mother, indeed I understand she never saw her again. She graduated with a first-class degree, posh accent, and my father. He'd fared a little better in a suburban family, living with a brother and two sisters in a three-bedroom semi. Like my mother he was bright, if not quite as bright as she, but he made up for that because he was prepared to work like a trojan to get where he wanted to be. They met in their first year and became a dream team, a dazzling power couple who didn't suffer fools, had their own secret language, and no apparent back story. I often wondered why they'd ever chosen to have a child, they never seemed natural parent material. There was no doubt I'd had a privileged upbringing; the best of everything, exclusive boarding school, designer wardrobe, a pony when I came back home for the holidays. Everything that money could buy, but I had been so damn lonely.

She'd been surprised when I called. I was desperate to get this visit over and done with but wanted to keep it low key. "Hey, Sandy," I said, "You around over the weekend, can I pop in?" I honestly didn't think they'd be around at such short notice, they were always talking about their hectic social life, although I did wonder whether they used that as an excuse for not seeing me too often, or maybe my mother just didn't like last-minute arrangements, but she surprised me.

"Darling, we'd love to see you. We're free all weekend, had a couple of things cancelled – we were going to be at David and Sally's, but David's come down with some sort of virus." I grinned to myself, she made it sound as if he'd done it just to be difficult.

"Brilliant, I'm so glad – not about David of course."

"Why the urgency?" she wanted to know. "Anything

wrong?" She was like a Jack Russell when it came to sniffing things out.

I went with a little white lie. "Just want to run a few things past you, finances and that, I've got some decisions to make." Then to change the subject, "And I knew you'd want to see pictures of Alice's wedding."

I could hear her smile over the phone. "Mmm, lovely girl, lawyer now, doing really well, isn't she?" Trust Sandy not to miss an opportunity for a dig. She knew my friends well, we had a lot of spare rooms and they'd come to stay often over the years. She'd taken a particular shine to Alice, and that law degree was the icing on the cake. As usual, I fell short because I'd opted out of law and hadn't wanted to join the family firm.

"How's the sleeping?" she asked, "Those rotten nightmares?"

I could feel another necessary white lie well on its way. "No, not for ages, probably grown out of them." For some reason her reaction to my night terrors had always been more exasperation than anything else, and she'd even taken me to see a child psychiatrist. He suggested the lucid dreams might be simply because I was highly intelligent with an overactive mind. Her solution was to make me work harder, keeping me busy with clubs at school and activities at home, giving me little time to think.

"Good to hear," she said now. "I'm not just having you 'pop' in though, come for the weekend. Will you make it for supper?"

"Should do, 7ish?"

"Right, see you then." She disconnected. I knew she knew there was something going on.

Arriving at the house I'd grown up in, on a beautiful late spring evening, and seeing it with a fresh eye, I realised just how intimidating it looked. It stood out even amongst the others in that exclusive Surrey enclave. I slid my window down at the imposing electric wrought iron gates designed to keep out unwelcome or uninvited visitors, and keyed the code. A spectacular example of Victorian Gothic architecture, the building before me looked as if it could be the perfect setting for a haunted horror movie. The gates silently opened up and I drove through and onto the sweeping drive. If the house wasn't picture perfect, the garden certainly made up for it, skilfully landscaped paths, a small lake, and a maze, carefully placed concealed grottos complete with rose-covered arbours, and pergolas. Our house never felt homely, but I loved our garden where I could always escape, and could count on not being interrupted for hours. Sandy had gradually changed the existing layout to her own interpretation of *The Secret Garden*, she even had a treasured first edition of the book, and it was those illustrations she worked from. Even as I drove, I was itching to abandon the car, step out and explore.

As I said, most of my childhood had been spent boarding, I only came home during the holidays. I'd never really understood why, when you had a child, you'd send them away for so much of their childhood, especially if your own experience had been so dysfunctional. Maybe it was because I spent so much time away that led to my relying more on friends than my parents for my emotional wellbeing, and I was often whisked away by one friend or another on their family holidays. It was refreshing if revelationary to see how other families behaved, and to note the lack of criticism levelled from mothers who seemed far more interested in slapping sun lotion on me than pointing out my swimsuit was getting too tight because I'd put on weight.

Some of the worst arguments between me and Sandy stemmed from me having to strip down to my underwear and get on the scales on a regular basis. She was obsessive about my weight, her own weight and in fact other people's weight, and she was constantly comparing me to my peers. Unsurprisingly the result was disordered eating which over teenage years deteriorated into a genuine eating disorder, until a very firm intervention by my best friends shook me into seeing sense and I hauled myself into a completely different way of thinking. Nowadays I ate healthily but well, and calorie-counting didn't come in to it.

There was no doubt that Sandy was a snob of the worst kind. Having dragged herself up from the very bottom rung, she didn't hesitate to look down her nose at anyone she'd passed on the way. She was convinced her dress, jewellery and manners gave the effortless impression she came from old money and would have died of humiliation had she realised they probably gave away far more than they concealed. I always felt she was a rather more glamorous version of Mrs Bouquet, except with her it was never a case of keeping up with, but rather always being a step or two ahead of the Joneses. The energy devoted to this was extraordinary, although she got bored easily, regularly changing her look. Her interior design style was very much Laurence Llewelyn-Bowen with an added touch of glitz and chintz. Nearly every room in the house was a migraine-inducing mismatch of clashing colours and patterns she liked to call eclectic. It was certainly responsible for pushing me towards my own cool, calm preferences, the very opposite of her chosen colour and chaos.

I hadn't lived at home for years now, but they still kept my room with its ensuite bathroom, and walk-in wardrobe. I loved my parents, but with the benefit of time away could more easily see that I valued and used possessions and surroundings as an emotional crutch as a direct result of my upbringing, taking my worldview from theirs. Perhaps it was the fact that they were only able to show affection in this way that caused the invisible yet impenetrable barrier I always felt stood between us.

Sandy was still in the garden when I arrived; the sun was strong and I knew she wasted no time when the weather was good. She wore oversized sunglasses and a baseball cap, looking far younger than her sixty-plus years. She looked very much like Goldie Hawn, with her bee-stung lips, blonde choppy highlights, and her size 6 figure which hadn't changed since her twenties. Consequently she'd retained all her clothes from previous decades, which were now deliciously vintage, and very on trend. Her walk-in wardrobe was a wonder to behold, and as a child I'd spent hours trying on shoes, hats, jewellery and jackets.

Fitness was important to my parents, they both played tennis, and were religiously regular gym attenders. They'd jet off with friends on a tennis jaunt at the drop of a hat, or head to a far-flung golf course so Geoff could play. Sandy was a collector as well, and the house was full of what she called precious collectables, although my feeling was they were anything but, and most of them would have been better off in the bin. But she did get pleasure from all of them; a typical example was her assortment of large, small and miniature pottery Staffordshire dogs, which were far better in her eyes than the real thing, which would have had a great time digging up her beautifully manicured lawn. I felt she was not so much a collector as a hoarder, possibly the legacy of a background with little or no possessions.

It was a while since I'd last visited my parents, so I wasn't surprised at the new cars sitting on the drive. There was a bright orange F-Type Jaguar, with Sandy's personal number plate, and I saw Geoff had a new style Bentley; they didn't believe in stinting themselves. Well, if we ran out of other things to talk about I could always get them to sing the praises of their new acquisitions.

Sandy looked up smiling from where she knelt by a flowerbed as I crunched down the gravelled path.

"Darling, lovely to see you, so pleased you're here. Thought I'd have a quick tidy up before Graham comes to do the garden." She looked sheepish, "I know, silly isn't it?" She was pushing something into her pocket.

"Don't bother hiding them," I said, "I thought you'd given up."

"Yes, well I have, it's just it's been a long week, and I had a horrendous time in court, couple of difficult cases. Don't tell Geoff but I really can't get along with vaping, oh it helps some of the time but it's not the same." I tended not to think of her having any vices, certainly not concealing them from Geoff. On the other hand, if she was planning to grow old disgracefully that could take a whole lot of pressure off me.

"Lips are sealed," I assured her with the appropriate gesture, then looking around. "It feels like an age since I was last here. Saw the new Jag – colour possibly a bit too subdued?"

She smiled. "I know, I couldn't resist, and yes you're right, it's been too long." She extracted a small tube from her pocket, and gave herself a quick mouth spray. "Don't want to give Geoff cause for suspicion. Trouble is we all lead such busy lives, don't we, but we'll make an effort to make visits more frequent." As she got to her feet, she gave me a quick once over. I knew there was nothing her eagle eye would miss, and sure enough;

"Darling, what *have* you been doing to yourself, you're looking a little rough round the edges. Working and partying too hard?" She'd long ago abandoned her cockney twang for cut-glass RP. Not waiting for an answer she linked her arm in mine, and we turned to continue up the drive. "We'll have to get you out in the sun this weekend, you really are looking pasty." She tutted, "And honestly, sweetheart, what *have* you done to your hair?" Then taking a step back to get a better look, she said, "And if you don't mind my saying, your skin hasn't been this bad since you were a teenager. Are you ill?" As I'd expected there were no holds barred – and we hadn't even got to the front door.

"Wow, Sandy," I said, "You certainly know how to make a girl feel good. Look, I know I need to sort myself out, maybe I'm deficient in something, I'll get a check-up but most likely I'm just tired, I certainly don't feel ill." I forestalled her before she could say anything else, "Where's Geoff? I want to say hello before supper." I knew she wasn't going to let the subject of my appearance drop, that wasn't her way, she'd get back to her running commentary later.

"In the chalet, I call it his man cave, and the physio is giving him a going over. Actually I'm not sure whether he really has hurt his back, lots more twinges apparently, or is just enjoying her undivided attention, you'll see what I mean." I laughed and headed for the chalet at the side of the house, but as I got near, could see through the window my half-dressed father laughing and chatting to a gorgeous looking woman of my own age. They hadn't noticed me and I made a snap decision that in fact I could wait till supper to say hello, swung on my heel and headed back to the house.

Later, sitting round the sturdy farmhouse table, pine-topped with grey painted legs and brightly mismatched cushions on the chairs, it was such a familiar setting that for a moment I couldn't imagine I'd ever been away. Sandy had given me a puzzled look when Geoff put his arms round me for a hug.

"Ellie, so fabulous to see you," he said.

I hugged him back. "Great to be here, and then for Sandy's benefit, I said, "I was going to say hello earlier and came to your man cave, but you were in the middle of your physio session and I didn't like to disturb you."

Geoff nodded, smiled absently and made himself busy pouring each of us a glass of high-end red wine. He had an amazing wine collection, and a magnificent cellar in which to store it – one of the benefits of a Victorian pile. Supper was healthy tossed salad, chicken breast and couscous, with homemade marinade, and I tucked in with enthusiasm, I was famished.

"Geoff, don't you think Ellie looks a little pale?" Sandy was back on course.

He glanced over. "Possibly, hadn't really noticed."

"There, I thought so." Sandy was triumphant. "Ellie, have you booked a holiday yet? Somewhere hot and luxurious is what I prescribe."

"Well, we went to the Yorkshire Moors for Alice's hen party, the weather was glorious, and I take vitamin D too," I offered.

She snorted, "*Yorkshire*! Why on earth go there, you needed to hop on a plane to somewhere exotic. I'm surprised Alice didn't insist."

"Alice did insist, she insisted on this country, she's cutting her carbon footprint." She gave me a sideways look; she was even less relaxed than normal, radiating nervous energy, I wasn't sure why.

"What about you?" I said, "Booked anything, another cruise?" They were cruise crazy, and loved nothing better than heading to and round the Caribbean. She nodded, although I don't think I had her full attention.

"Probably the Seychelles, with Martin and Samantha, you know, from Tennis Club. After this last winter we're all desperate for some sunshine, aren't we, darling?" Geoff nodded in agreement as she continued, probably because he knew it was never worthwhile disagreeing when she was in full flow. As I rose to clear away the plates and fill the dishwasher, I noticed Sandy, usually a light drinker, perhaps conscious of her family history, had tonight emptied her second glass of wine, and now I thought about it her speech was slightly slurred.

"No, no, leave that, darling, sit down, you're here to relax, Geoff?" and she passed him my glass to refill. I wondered briefly whether she had in fact started drinking before I got there. I retrieved the glass with a smile.

"No, I've already had more than enough, if I'm not careful I'll fall asleep before I've even got to my bed." I'd talk to them tomorrow, I decided. "Do you mind if I call it a night? Head's throbbing."

"Of course, darling, we can catch up properly tomorrow," she said, unconsciously echoing my own thought as we said our goodnights.

I felt a lot more with it the following morning, and after a light breakfast, we went out to spend time in the garden. I'd brought a good book with me and settled down in one of my favourite quiet spots while my mother went back to whatever plant pottering she'd been doing before, and my father with a muttered excuse about filing disappeared to the chalet. I knew I couldn't put off forever the conversation I'd come down here to have. Sandy was still restless, wearing a large floppy sunhat, doing a fair old bit of staccato snipping with the secateurs, muttering to herself when she came across a particularly stubborn growth, and dead-heading a lot of roses. After a couple of hours of that she headed for the house, reappearing with picnic basket and blanket, ready for an al fresco lunch, and my father in tow.

It was as we started on what she'd prepared that she unintentionally handed me the opening I needed. "Ellie, you haven't said how things are going at work, still hitting those targets?"

"Actually," I said, taking a deep breath, "That's one of the things I wanted to talk to you about, and I'm glad you're sitting down!" I laughed nervously as they both immediately looked alarmed and exchanged a look. The glare of the sun mercilessly revealed lines on faces I hadn't noticed last night, and I saw they were both looking older. I was struck by a flash of remorse; I really didn't want to upset them.

"Spit it out then," Geoff said,

"Right, well, I've handed in my notice."

"At work?" said Geoff.

"Where else?" I said. "I'm officially on garden leave." They were silent, shocked, both looking at me in a way that was usually enough to turn my legs to jelly. I was so relieved to have actually got the news out that I didn't feel as bad as I usually did.

Sandy spoke first, and needless to say she'd immediately grabbed the wrong end of the stick. "You've been head-hunted, haven't you, I knew it would happen sooner or later, where are going?"

"Nope," I said, "Not that, not a head-hunter in sight. Actually I don't have any career plans at the moment, and I'm moving out of London."

"It's a health issue, isn't it, what aren't you telling us?"

Sandy took off her sunhat and laid it on the grass next to her. “You said you were feeling fine.”

“I am feeling fine, I’ve just been working under such a lot of pressure, I’m stressed out, and tired.” Of course I also knew the extra burden on me was my dreams, not to mention Hettie and all the Whitby weirdness, but there was no way I could even begin to lay that out for them. “I just feel I need to leave city living, it’s not doing me any good, actually I’m moving out to the country, an 18th-century cottage just outside a sweet little village. I came across it when I was away with the girls.” This time there was no disguising the distraught look that passed between them.

“So, let me get this straight,” said Geoff, who usually waited for Sandy to voice thoughts first, “You went to Yorkshire for a weekend, saw a pretty cottage, and on the spur of the moment are now making a massive life change?” I didn’t say anything. “Come on,” he said, “It makes no sense. Look, we’ve all been to some amazing places over the years, places we’ve loved, but we haven’t suddenly decided to give up everything and move there.”

Sandy took up the baton; she’d picked up the hat again and was agitatedly fanning herself. “Ellie, what is wrong with you? We’ve given you everything money can buy, made sure you had a first-class education, now you say you’re throwing it all away on some crazy pipe dream, and Yorkshire of all places.”

Geoff, usually the calmer of the two, was right there with her on the indignation front. “Why don’t you just get a second home, a holiday home, and if you don’t want to think about going abroad, Cornwall would be a far better option. How about Rock, lots of our friends have holiday places there?"

I shook my head smiling, "I've made my mind up, I'm afraid." Sandy weighed in again, "I can understand you might be bored with the job, that happens. But what about re-training, joining the family firm – we could sponsor you." I appreciated that she was trying, but I honestly couldn't think of anything worse than spending my working life under her eye, and I was surprised to feel how much my confidence had grown over the last few months. This was my life after all, I wasn't ten years old, I wasn't going to be bullied. I held up my hand.

"Stop it, both of you," I said, "I've given my notice in, I've left my job, and my apartment is on the market. I have no intention of changing my mind. I love the cottage I've bought. It needs total renovation but I'm looking forward to that. I want you both to come and see it, so you get the benefit of the before and after." But taking in their expressions of raw despair, I was bewildered. "Honestly, you couldn't look more upset if I'd told you I was planning a bank heist." There was a brief weighted pause before Sandy spoke again, "I can't believe this. After all we have done for you, Ellie, the time and effort we've invested. You've let us down terribly." She glanced at Geoff, "I think I speak for both of us when I say I don't think we'll be rushing to visit you there, anytime soon."

"I'm sorry you feel like that." I was holding down my temper with an effort. "But perhaps you're forgetting I'm thirty years old, not a child anymore. The cottage is paid for with money I've earned. I'm not asking for any financial help from you, although I am and always will be grateful for everything you've done for me." I stopped for breath then continued more quietly. "I'd like, but don't need your approval, and I certainly would like your blessing. But if you can't manage that it doesn't change anything. My mind's made up and as long as I'm happy about that, that's all that matters..." I stopped. I don't know which of the three of us was more surprised at the clarity of my statement. There was a tight, uncomfortable silence, and then my mother started to silently collect up the plates. The picnic was over.

We didn't really speak for the rest of the afternoon and evening, polite pleasantries were passed and nobody was rude but there was no mistaking the displeasure radiating from both of them. They could see it was futile to try to change my mind; after all they'd brought me up, so knew better than anyone else the extent of my obstinacy once I had an idea in my head. By the time I went up to my room after dinner I felt I'd gone twenty rounds in a boxing ring, and the chilly goodnights from my parents made me feel less like a daughter and more like an unwelcome B&B guest.

Thankfully, the next morning, after a long mercifully dreamless sleep, I felt surprisingly refreshed and certainly relieved. I'd broken the news so that apprehension was no longer weighing me down. There was no doubt their response had riled me, but I understood, this was just who they were. I loved them in my own way, and they loved me in theirs. But this was a new era, me taking control of my own life and decisions. That this in no way slotted into their regimented lifestyle meant they were way out of their comfort zone, completely baffled by what they saw as a lunatic, un-thought-through decision. But this weekend I'd glimpsed chinks in their armour, so maybe their life wasn't so perfect after all. I also reflected that if they hadn't coped well with what I'd told them, goodness only knows how they'd have coped with the so much more I hadn't. Today was a new day however, and I'd survived to tell the tale.

CHAPTER 10

Checking my phone now I was back at my apartment, after the traumatic weekend with my parents, I saw there was a hive of activity on the WhatsApp 'Wedding News', and Oli had also set up an 'Ellie's Leaving Do'. I'd deliberately left my phone at home during a mind-clearing run along the towpath. The weather was extremely un-British at the moment with temperatures higher than Spain, and I was taking full advantage. Knowing I only had a short time left as a Londoner had sharpened my appreciation. Clearing my mind of conflicting thoughts with running and walking had helped and I was making the most of all that was on offer in the area. I'd lived here for a good while, but never really had the opportunity to explore. Spending so much time outdoors was good for me, I could see my skin tone improving little by little. I knew I'd been ignoring my health issues, and was determined to get a recommendation for a good dermatologist and perhaps a trichologist too, to get my skin and hair issues sorted. But today my thoughts were on Hettie and the supernatural experience at Whitby Harbour. The dreams that had haunted me seemed to be fading and I certainly hadn't had any more weird experiences. I'd spent so many years disturbed by the lucid dreams and knew I should be delighted they'd ceased, but I couldn't deny I was anxious to see Hettie again, learn more from her. She'd been absent since that last blurred dream, and I was struggling now to remember just when that was. On the other hand, was it possible that all the recent happenings were down to something as simple as overwork, not enough healthy eating and lack of downtime?

My phone was an unwelcome intruder at this point in time but I realised I couldn't put off answering the WhatsApp messages indefinitely, the girls would worry. Returning from a run, I resolved to shower later – deal with messages first. Putting on a leisure suit after I made myself a coffee, I poured the frothed milk, barista style, on top, and made my way out onto the balcony, coffee in one hand, phone in the other. Don't get me wrong, I love speaking to my friends, but I knew my news would call forth a whole load of questions, and probably plenty of objections.

I went through the messages, looking out over the river where locals, tourists, and students were all enjoying the sunshine. I wasn't going to suggest another get-together for the time being, as all the girls had work commitments, and Alice would have a pile of stuff to deal with now she'd got back from her honeymoon. Of course, I couldn't indefinitely avoid sharing my news, but maybe virtually was better than in person. First though, I'd reply to Oli's messages, all of which had come in over the last few days:

Oli: Hey girlfriend, hope you're enjoying life. I am organising your leaving do.

Oli: You ok? I messaged two days ago – you usually come back straight away.

Me: Sorry my lovely, been out and about, phone ran out of charge.

Oli: Phew! Had me soooo worried. How are you my darling? Loving life out of the rat race, or bored stiff?

Me: You are so, so, funny. Not at all bored, best decision ever made.

Oli: Well I think it's the worst thing ever. Office isn't the same without you.

Me: You'll see me soon enough, and don't forget you're coming to visit and see the cottage, you can even have input on the renovations, you're great at that, much better than me.

Oli: No use you trying to make me feel better. I am devastated, you kept me sane. Doesn't sound like you're ready to change your mind though?

Me: Too right!

Oli: OK. Party. 2 weeks today? All the guys are good with that date. You?

Me: Fine, have to brush off my glad rags, haven't

dressed up for ages, no wait, of course there was the wedding, otherwise tracksuit and trainers. How are things there?

Oli: Not the same without your beautiful face, that's for sure!

Me: Too kind! Can't wait to see you, where we going?

Oli: Meet at our usual wine bar. 6.30, and don't be late!

Me: Excited, see you there.

Oli: Expect a messy night! Ciao Babe!

Then I moved on to the girls, to find their messages had piled up too:

Alice: Hey lovelies, back from my honeymoon – you're all awesome, best bridesmaids ever, thank you, you made the day perfect.

Lizzie: Still buzzing, we had an awesome time, and Ali you were the most radiant bride I've ever seen, we all nearly wept buckets, runny mascara only thing stopping us. Loved the string quartet, it was a spectacular day.

Sarah: What she said! Mrs M, you were stunning, and thank heaven no last minute dress hitches – think I was more nervous than you.

Alice: I knew there wouldn't be, your designs were perfect, and you're far too bossy to have missed anything that wasn't right. But yes it did go smoothly didn't it?

Sarah: Pure magic, and the Ceilidh was something else. Still have the bruises. And Robbie scrubs up well doesn't he, we all love a man in a kilt, especially a designer one!

Alice: Sorry about bruises, it was energetic wasn't it, shame the kilt doesn't come out more often.

Lizzie: Dying to see pictures, can you send? I know you'll have a ton of work but at least send some though – just to be getting on with.

Alice: Course I will, but you're right, been like a madhouse here since I got back.

Sarah: How was the Highlands honeymoon, hope the camper didn't leak, and bet you moaned about lack of creature comforts.

Alice: Don't mock – it was great. Bit cosy, but great, and so remote, no-one else to worry about and we were dead lucky with the weather.

Lizzie: Sounds like you're turning into an earth angel.

Alice: Matter of fact, and don't laugh, we loved being out there so much we're going to buy our own camper.

Lizzie: Well, who's a hippy chick then? Blimey you'll be doing Glastonbury next, and don't bother asking – my answer would be NO WAY!

Alice: There's a surprise! But seriously, it felt a world away from normal life. Anyone heard from Ellie, she's usually welded to her phone and first to answer.

Sarah: Hey, Ellie, you out there?

Lizzie: You ok Ellie?

Me: I've been giving my phone a rest believe it or not, that's why I didn't get back sooner. Just got in from a 10 mile run along the Thames! Incredible weather, Ali you must have brought it back with you. Glad the honeymoon was great.

Alice: Running? Why aren't you at work? What's going on?

Me: Funny you talking about a low maintenance lifestyle, hope you're all sitting down. I've got news I've been saving for after the wedding.

Sarah: Good? Bad? Promotion? Sack? Out with it.

Lizzie: You've met the love of your life!

Me: Ha ha! None of the above.

Alice: Don't keep us in suspense, you're not ill are you? I knew something was going on. Have you seen a specialist?

Me: Making an appointment, but listen, I am taking steps to make myself feel better.

Sarah: OMG, what have you done?

Lizzie: If you don't start talking, I'm going to come over and shake it out of you!

Me: It's just I didn't want to take any focus off the wedding.

Alice: I'm going to start SCREAMING!!

Me: Ok, I've given my notice at work. I'm on garden leave! I'm moving to the countryside – there, it's out!

Lizzie: But you LOVE your job. I don't believe this. You love your apartment too.

Me: I do, but it's on the market now – bidding war going on, deadline next Friday, price keeps going up!

Alice: You haven't said where you're going? And what about a job?

Me: Going to take my time looking, but I am about to complete on a cottage, in Eastcombe. We actually passed there on one of our jaunts in Yorkshire, I spotted the for sale sign and went for it.

Alice: I KNEW something was going on, you've been so quiet. Knew you were tired and not feeling great, but this, this is crazy!!

Sarah: Alice you can say that. Is it on Rightmove, can we look? Is it gorgeous?

Me: Yes, on Rightmove, defo not gorgeous at the moment, lots of work to be done.

Alice: ELLIE WHY?? You love the buzz of city life. Have you thought this through?

Me: As the saying goes, "If you never try, you'll never know." Haven't felt right for a while, rundown, head all over the place. A huge change will do me the world of good – and what's the worst that can happen?

Sarah: You have been off recently, we've been worried. You really think this is the answer?

Lizzie: Hey girls, silver lining, at least we'll have

somewhere different to come and holiday with you, we love Yorkshire – is there room for us all?

Me: Have a look on Rightmove before you pack any bags! I'll probably be renting while the cottage gets some TLC. And of course I'll have room – when it's done.

Alice: Don't want to be the cold-water pourer, I know you loved Yorkshire too, but leaving London? Is that really the right thing?

Lizzie: It's amazing news, but we are all a bit stunned, not sure how long you'll survive in the countryside.

Alice: What about work? Will you do something totally new?

Me: Not sure. Just going to go with the flow. First I'll project manage the cottage, but time off will do me good.

Alice: You know we've all got your back, just hope we don't have to pick up the pieces when it all goes pear shaped. Sorry, Ellie, just worried, and what about that check-up appt?

Sarah: Exciting times! But agree with Alice, get that appt made. And good luck!

Lizzie: Can't wait to see your new place. Love you so much, just want you to be happy.

Me: I swear I'll keep you updated, and take care of my health. Can't wait to see wedding pictures. I'll share the ones on my phone.

Alice: Make sure you and your phone don't lose contact with us again!

Well that went, if not well, at least better than expected – probably because I omitted the real reason for the move, I'm not sure what reaction I'd have got then. I was just relieved it had been texts all the way, because face to face, Alice had a way of flushing things out like nobody else. I needed space and time to get used to my new life, and more importantly to find the hidden space at the cottage that held Hettie's secrets, if there was one? Maybe one day I'd be ready to tell the girls the real reason for the move, but for now enough was enough. I also had to admit there was the stubborn side of me that was determined to prove them wrong, make a huge success of this move. After all I was doing this for my own well-being, as well as yearning to learn what Hettie had to teach me. To do all that I had to follow my new path to my new life.

CHAPTER 11

The deadline for my apartment sale passed, and sure enough, Brett the estate agent called late Friday morning.

"Well, it's been pretty fierce, never seen anything quite like it. You've sold at a whopping £500k higher than your asking price!"

"Wow, that's taken my breath away. Who bought it?"

"Last-minute bid last night, mystery buyer apparently, they want all fixtures and fittings included. They want to stay anonymous, that's their strict stipulation, their identity will only be revealed to the solicitors."

"How strange, but that's OK isn't it?" Perfect that they also wanted all the fixtures and fittings, now I wouldn't have to worry about what to do with my stuff, none of which would be right for the cottage. "That's a fantastic result though, thank you, let's get things moving before they have a chance to change their mind!"

"Of course, then all down to the solicitors. Rest assured though, we'll keep chasing from our end."

"Thanks again, Brett, you've made my day."

With a broad grin, I moved to the balcony, to see what the weather was doing. It had started to drizzle so I thought I might just spend the day chilling out. My leaving do was tonight, and I wanted to enjoy it. Lying on my bed, and luxuriating in laziness I picked up a novel, *The Woman in White*, by Wilkie Collins. Sarah had given it to me when were away, along with a rave review. Victorian Gothic literature was not my usual thing, but I'd give it a go. I hadn't managed to finish a book for ages, so it was good now to have some me-time. Then I picked myself up on that because from now on it was all going to be about me, and Hettie of course. My mind wandered to the cottage; maybe a large bookcase in one of the bedrooms on which could go all the books I'd now have time to read. I'd already started decorating in my mind's eye. I planned to enhance some of the original features, exposing as much stone and wood as possible, although not quite back to the basic earthiness of Hettie's time. I'd already accumulated a pile of country living and property renovation magazines, and they were giving me inspiration aplenty.

I read happily for a while, enjoying the book, and then decided I'd take a break, spend some time tidying myself up after my weeks of living more naturally. I ran a bubble bath, and coming to the end of the bottle, decided I was going to replace it with something far less pricey. Priorities had changed for me, I was building a whole new set of values alongside a growing sense of freedom. With the sale of my current home, it felt as if layers of my old life were being peeled away layer by onion-like layer. I didn't know what the future held, but that in itself was exciting.

The purchase of Lavender Cottage was going well. I'd started looking for local tradespeople, particularly a stonemason for all that Yorkshire stone. I was desperate to properly search the property too, before any builder set foot in it, although I was hopeful Hettie would make contact before then and give me some more clues. In her absence I'd just have to put my own brain to work, as the cottage wasn't that big, and there couldn't be that many hiding places.

I did feel that things I'd been worrying about were easing off a great deal. I'd made peace with the girls, and after the initial surprise they seemed genuinely happy that I was happy.

There was no doubt life was getting a little less complicated. Bath ready, Zero 7 on the playlist, Jo Malone candles lit and a drop of Neom elixir oil added to the water. I poured myself an indulgent glass of chardonnay, and I was all set. I hadn't been near a beautician for weeks, and I knew some of my ex-colleagues would notice a change, but in reality it didn't bother me that much. I had a sense of calm, knowing I didn't have to impress, a new lightness in my heart, and overall control of my life. The icing on my cake was a message that came through from the girls, wishing me the best for tonight. With a sigh of contentment, I slipped into the bubbles.

I spent far too long in there, and although I was thoroughly relaxed my skin had gone prune-like from the water and I knew it was still very dry. But I'd come to another decision, I'd see how living in the countryside improved my health. I didn't feel ill, and my stamina was OK for running, maybe I'd postpone booking in to see anyone. The immediate issue now was making myself look half decent for a good night out. I'd booked a cab for 6.00 to get me to the wine bar for 6.30. I was looking forward to going out for a change and socialising, I'd become a little antisocial of late. I slathered my skin with some luxurious body cream, and a few sprays of Chanel. I'd found a pretty dress that would work for a night out, though I wasn't sure how ready I was for high heels, I'd have to get used to them again. I spent most of my time now in leisure gear and trainers. Curling my hair, and putting on makeup, a little heavier than usual, I felt a lot more glam, and sent a selfie for the girls captioned 'The girl still scrubs up well'.

The taxi arrived and I reached for my leather jacket – the weather had cooled a little – grabbed my clutch bag with essentials, phone, lippy and debit card, and headed down. Traffic was dreadful and I reached the wine bar ten minutes late, I could see Oli and other colleagues were already there, including Sophie. I knew she for one was delighted to see the back of me, and guessed she'd have something to say to the others the next day about my appearance, but I'd just smile sweetly because tonight was my night. I don't know why but she'd taken an instant dislike to me, must be jealousy, we'd never clicked. Simon had turned up too, which was surprising because whilst constantly telling us what a team player he was, he rarely mixed socially. Funny what you see once you're on the outside looking in, viewing group dynamics with a more impartial eye. Sure enough, Sophie gave me a quick once-over, and a "Daaaarling, you look amazing!" which convinced neither of us, saying, "How are you getting on, it's so good to see you!" and we did the requisite mwah, mwah without touching each other's cheek.

"All going well thanks," I said. There are some people you can talk to for hours, Sophie wasn't one of them, our conversations had always been stilted. Keen to get away, I started moving towards Oli. "Excuse me, Sophie, won't you, just need to catch up with Oli to say thanks for organising all this." As I made my way over, Sophie had already moved on. "Oli, so sorry I'm late, traffic tonight is appalling."

"No worries, doll, you look divine, not working's certainly working for you!" There was a hint of waspishness, but that was Oli for you, he didn't mean it.

"Thanks, I'd forgotten what it took to be presentable, been living in sweats."

"Well you're here now and do I have a fun evening in store." Standing next to Oli was a stunning guy, mid-twenties, blond cropped hair, and deep denim blue eyes. "Ellie, this is Zac." I smiled and shook hands, hiding any disappointment that this was Oli's new squeeze.

"Great to meet you."

"You too, Ellie, Oli's told me all about you, he's missing you like crazy."

"You'll both have to come over and see my new place once it's renovated," I said.

"Brilliant." He placed a possessive arm over Oli's shoulders, and I knew from the way Oli pointedly didn't meet my eye that this guy wouldn't be around for long.

"I'd better do some mingling," I said, "Oli, you've got such a fabulous group together, can't thank you enough."

He smiled smugly. "Don't get too settled, we're moving on shortly, I've found the perfect venue, you'll know why when you see it." We spent about another half hour catching up, making small talk and taking in a few more glasses of wine, and then Oli indicated we were ready for the next stage. Mike, my old driver, had been invited and offered Oli and Zac a lift along with me, so we'd get there before the others. That way Oli could be sure I had time to savour my surprise, whilst checking everything was in place.

To my surprise Mike drew up outside one of the historic style London pubs along the Thames. "You get out, guys, and I'll go and park." Following Oli as he stepped out of the car, I reached out for his arm, as I could tell my heels weren't suited to the cobbled stone. Once anchored, I looked around. Beer kegs and metal tables were set out for smokers, there was lots of litter, and an oppressively heavy smell of stale beer.

"Is this the right place, Oli?" Many of these areas in London had been gentrified, and I knew this was an area which had undergone some regeneration recently, but it was still along the less salubrious section of the Thames.

"Darling, haven't you noticed the sign?" Looking where he was pointing, I saw a plaque asserting there'd been a tavern on this site since 1520, making it the oldest tavern on the river, and then I laughed as I took in the pub sign. 'The Prospect of Whitby'.

"Couldn't resist it, my lovely," Oli said smugly. "Homage to your Yorkshire move. Don't worry, that's not all, there are lots of treats in store for you, and I promise it's better inside than out."

"Bless you," I smiled at him. "I'm sure it'll be lush if you've had anything to do with it!" I shivered, feeling the temperature had dropped. "Come on, let's get inside." Zac held the door for us and we both hurried into the warmth, although I still felt chilled through, and thoroughly uneasy. For a moment I felt as if someone was behind me. I thought it was Zac following us in but he'd already moved ahead to catch up with Oli, and the rest of the gang hadn't yet arrived. I shrugged, and looked around; it was all dark panelling, low wooden beams, the tourists must love it. The floor was flagstone with beer kegs utilised as bar stools around the pewter-topped bar. There was indeed a heavy dose of old-world charm, steeped in history, and obviously little had changed here over the centuries. The guy behind the bar greeted Oli warmly, and ushered us towards the back of the building into a private room leading onto a balcony with chairs and tables overlooking the river.

"I'll come and take drink orders, when the rest of your party arrive. No smoking out here but there's an area at the front for those who want." Oli had gone to town, and then well over the top too with the seaside theme. A sweet kiosk had been set up in the corner of the room with an assortment of old-fashioned sweets in glass jars, sticks of rock, mini candy floss, and toffee apples on sticks. He'd also hired an ice cream vendor, now setting up in another corner, ready to dole out cornets with flakes, and as if all that wasn't enough, a delicious smell of donuts filled the air.

"This is incredible, Scarborough Fair springs to mind, remember the song? Oli, you are such a sweetie." The rest of the partygoers were drifting in now, exclaiming in surprise and delight while Oli worked the room giving out kiss-me-quick hats, tacky, but fun! Finally, he called everyone's attention with a theatrical throat clearing.

"Just a few words," then to laughter, "*Only* a few, you cheeky lot. As you can see I wanted to send our Ellie off with a real seaside theme – what the *hell* are you *doing* moving to Yorkshire, Ellie, we all miss you so much." Murmurs of agreement, although I noted Sophie didn't open her mouth. Oli went on, "Despite your daft decision we do wish you the very best for your future life. Now enough from me, make sure you've got a drink; fish and chips will be right out and there are, as you see, lots of sweet treats. Fill your boots. Now, Ellie, has the general gorgeousness of all this struck you dumb?" To a round of applause and shaking my head I moved forward, feeling surprisingly emotional.

"Thank you so much all of you for coming tonight, and, Oli, what can I say? How you managed to pull all this together, I'll never know, it's just sensational." At which point I paused for breath and Oli swept across the room with the biggest bouquet of flowers, and a few beautifully wrapped packages.

Seeing my eyes fill with tears, he announced, "OK, enough talking or we'll get maudlin, we're all ravenous, let's go."

I knew I should have a bite to eat to soak up the alcohol and maybe some of the emotion, and right on cue trays of paper-coned fish and chips arrived looking and smelling delicious. Oli's choice of 90s dance music, with which he was obsessed, was perfect in that setting and although the room wasn't massive, we all managed to squash in. My first dance was with Mike whose moves were as smooth as his driving. He'd offered to see me home safe and sound, so wasn't drinking tonight. Probably a good thing, I reflected, as I was feeling more than a little wasted, needed a knight in shining armour to keep an eye on me, and he was one of the good guys.

Towards the end of the night, I nipped to the ladies for a quick freshen up after all the dancing, and wash my sticky hands after filling my face with all the sweet treats. The heating obviously didn't extend to the Ladies and I shivered as I put on lippy and ran fingers through my hair before making my way back through the pub to the smokers' area. I wasn't a heavy smoker but did enjoy the occasional social cigarette, and usually carried some with me even though I was well aware most people had given up or were vaping. I spotted Rob, one of the senior execs, and seeing me he came over to offer a light.

"Ellie, my darling, looking gorgeous tonight."

"Thanks, Rob. How are you, how's things at work?"

"Same old, same old. But you, my lovely, complete life change?"

"Suppose so, all a bit surreal at the moment. I've sold my apartment, so full steam ahead now." I smiled at him; we'd always had a spark between us, although I didn't mix business with pleasure, and anyway he was married. We watched the Thames flow beneath us reflecting the inky black sky towards which our cigarette smoke curled lazily. Earlier drizzle had stopped and clouds had cleared, so we could see some stars and the full moon.

"Beautiful night," I murmured. I could see Rob's lips moving as he answered but couldn't hear his reply. And then with shocking suddenness I was enveloped by an acrid mixture of smoke and dense black fog Londoners used to call a pea-souper. For a moment I couldn't see a thing, but then as the thick fog cleared, Rob had disappeared, nowhere to be seen. I looked around me, it was broad daylight now, the sky clear, I guessed late morning. I slowly turned to face the pub, everything was slightly out of focus somehow, but it looked much the same although the sign now proclaimed it The Devil's Tavern. I was dimly aware of people rushing hither and thither on the cobbles, gesturing in animated conversation or angry dispute, strange though, I couldn't hear a thing. The usual bustling sounds of London, planes overhead, chaotic traffic noise and emergency service sirens constantly whizzing by, all gone. But then as the scene around me came into clear focus I heard the droning sound of human noise, church bells chiming in the distance. As I tried to attract the attention of passers-by, one thing was certain, they could neither see nor hear me, they looked straight through me as if I was a ghost.

I moved slowly through the front door of the pub, the foul smell hitting me hard, a mixture of sweat, stale ale, and that unmistakeable sewage smell, a combination of river water and God knows what else. A shiver ran down my spine; the atmosphere inside matched the darkness of the decor, dark and slightly menacing. Nothing much had changed other than candlelight replacing electric bulbs. The Georgian panelling absorbed what light there was, and sawdust had been kicked into small dirty piles on the uneven flagstone floor by passing boots.

Nautical decorations gave a nod to visiting sailors, a group of whom were crowded and hunched over playing cards, exchanging coins and curses, while a couple of them passed something between them under the table, goodness only knows what that was. Most of the drinkers were obviously the worse for wear, a group laughing raucously as they helped themselves to roughly made pies on the bar, and in the corner a couple of women were shrieking at each other, their shrillness rising until a man went over to pull them sharply apart. The door which had led to our party room was open and I could see straight through to where it seemed a cock fight was taking place, two underfed, bloodied birds tearing viciously at each other. I turned away swiftly; the movement in the tavern had slowed, nobody could see me but there was no doubt the atmosphere had changed uncomfortably as if all were aware of something unnatural taking place.

I made my way back outside, although the atmosphere was almost as choking as that inside because so many men were pipe smoking. A couple of women leant against the wall near the door, powdered white faces not disguising blemished skin with lips a sad slash of scarlet, as they cast eyes around for business. There didn't seem much chance of that, most of the drinkers being well into their stride. One of the men had a foam moustache, wiped it with an already filthy sleeve and succeeded only in spreading it over his face. Another missed his mouth and sloshed ale down his front to general hilarity. Grubby, shoeless urchins with sooty faces were begging and being angrily shooed away. With shock I focused on a young girl, about twelve or thirteen I thought; dressed only slightly better than the other children, she was looking around, waiting for someone. It was a younger Hettie, I was positive, she looked straight at me, and for just a few seconds I was sure she'd seen me.

I called desperately, "Hettie, it's Ellie, can you see me?" but she didn't respond. I was frustrated, it was futile yet I had so many questions, like what was she doing in London? How had she then made her way to Yorkshire? Maybe it was on one of the ships from London? A passenger or a stowaway? But her escape from this life to Yorkshire hadn't brought her any luck if my drowning dream was anything to go by. A rough-looking character emerged unsteadily from the pub, seized her arm in a vice-like grip and they disappeared into the milling crowd. I tried to follow, but swiftly lost sight of her although I continued in the same direction hoping to spot her again.

It seemed this area of London had been aiming for gentrification even back then, but there was no doubt it was working against the odds with drunken sailors, prostitutes, crooks and beggars. Everyone smelt different, and not in a good way. The crowd seemed to be moving with intention towards a certain point, and there was a feeling of anticipation as if they all knew something I didn't and were waiting. The stench was indescribable; open sewers from which I swiftly averted my eyes ran alongside the cobbled streets, and into the river. I looked out over the water. In my time it had its own unique smell, not always pleasant, but now the river was putrid enough to make you gag. It was packed with boats and larger ships, a constant stream of men and young boys loading and unloading goods from smaller boats ferrying back and forth between ships and shore, although goodness knows how they knew which goods were going where. I'd been slipping through gaps in the crowd. I knew they couldn't see me but I wondered if they sensed anything out of the ordinary as I passed. I wanted to see what was holding their attention. When I did, I instantly regretted it. A bedraggled man was hanging lifeless on the wooden gallows, and then like a blow to the stomach which nearly doubled me up in distress, I saw the executioner sever and hold up the dead man's hand, I knew what I was looking at, I'd seen a so-called Hand of Glory, at Hettie's cottage – protection for the household. I turned away quickly; I couldn't bear to see any more.

Still shaking, I dashed from the execution site and the baying crowd, avoiding hooves of horses as they pulled roughly-made wooden wagons that didn't look as if they'd last the journey, and stepping round piles of steaming manure. Unused to walking for so long on cobbles, my balance was unsound, and I screamed when a cat-sized rat crossed my path. As the wind changed direction, the unmistakeable aroma of urine hit me, overriding everything else. One of the big ships, 'Pride of Whitby' was anchored a short way from shore and was being loaded with barrels, *London Urine* stencilled on the side. Well that explained the smell both here and in Whitby – a urine trade, I didn't even want to think how that worked, the assault of repulsive smells was almost unbearable.

The boxes and crates being loaded and unloaded were followed by hordes of scavenging children, eager to get hands on whatever they could, as delighted with a lump of coal as with an apple. No childhood, just a fight to survive, I could see this was an era where swiftness and cunning could mean the difference between life and death. Sickened, I turned into one of the tight alleys running off the main street. I knew this area, the East End of London had always enjoyed a dubious reputation, and now I was watching the thriving black market in goods stolen from the ships. Women in ragged dresses and filthy pinafores were gutting fish, sorting fruit and vegetables, grabbing items brought by the children, examining then passing them along for a few coins. Organised chaos in a backdrop of bedlam, and probably all of it illegal. I moved on amongst the filth, misery and occasional violence, desperate for another glimpse of the little girl who was Hettie, then my sadness was swamped as the thick fog once again descended upon and around me, and everything went black.

Coming to, I could hear a voice faint but gradually increasing in volume. "Ellie, Ellie, can you hear me?" I could feel a light tapping on my face, as I gradually opened my eyes to a crowd around me. Mike, Rob, and some of my old colleagues were anxiously surrounding me. I knew exactly what had just happened, another time shift, the trigger seemed to be any link with Whitby – the name of the pub was The Prospect of Whitby – or was it Hettie? I didn't think this would work as an explanation to put people's minds at rest. I realised I was lying on Mike's raincoat, and now he helped me to sit up, leaning against a barrel.

"Young lady, it's about time I got you home – a bit too much celebrating I think…"

"God, Ellie, you gave me the shock of my life, just dropping down like that, you didn't even pass out completely, kept calling out for someone called Hettie." Rob did indeed look shaken. "And you've been out for over ten minutes now."

"Who the hell's Hettie?" Mike's hand was still on my shoulder as if he expected me to topple over again at any minute.

"I am," I said. Mike and Rob exchanged a look.

"Just how much have you had tonight?" Rob said. I pulled myself together with a gargantuan effort and gave what I hoped was a light laugh,

"Don't be silly, I'm just having you on. I do occasionally faint, nothing to worry about, low blood pressure and yes, almost certainly too much alcohol. Sorry." Naturally that was the only explanation they were going to get, I could hardly say I'd stayed in the past a little longer than I had last time. Although a little freaked out, I'd had an awesome experience, but it was certainly not for sharing. They'd be hitting 999 and I'd be checked all over for goodness knows what, maybe even sectioned under the Mental Health Act!

Leaning on Mike's arm, with Rob on the other side, I rose to my feet, preoccupied with what I'd learnt about Hettie's poverty in London, reflecting on just how she eventually wound up in Yorkshire when she fled the sordid city. I needed to get home, to think properly. But I knew Mike was an East End boy, and as he drove me back, I thought maybe there were stories he could tell me.

CHAPTER 12

September – Lavender Cottage

The sale on my London apartment had gone through really quickly, and the mystery buyer was keen to complete on the sale as soon as possible, but obviously the cottage was in no state yet for me to move in. Reluctant to pay extortionate rent in London while I waited, I brought forward the move to Yorkshire and rented a bijou apartment on a short-term lease overlooking the River Esk in Whitby. I loved where I was. I'd already seen Sammy the Seal and could have spent hours watching the grace of long-necked cormorants as they dived for fish. The North Yorkshire Moors historic train was just across the river, its shrill whistle carrying on the wind and its curling steam painting the sky as it passed.

I'd exchanged my Mercedes for a far more practical and as yet mud-unsullied Land Rover Discovery currently parked outside my temporary apartment, and I knew driving that I'd feel completely confident in the snow.

Thankfully all the fixtures and fittings had been sold with the apartment, and I had very few personal items. I'd kept my computer bag, bulging with technology and all the accessories that go with that. I also had a couple of cases full of clothes and had invested in some good quality autumn and winter gear, which I knew I'd get far more wear out of than any of my designer stuff. Power suits, and skimpy, bling dresses for a night on the town were going to be surplus to requirements, and I planned a clear-out. The local charity shops didn't know yet, but they were in for a windfall.

Both the weather and the leaves were starting to turn, and the chill in the air confirmed it was indeed colder in the north. One of the major lessons learnt in my lifestyle change was that in the future I'd probably need far less in the way of possessions, and I was excited and impatient now to start my new life. It was a great adventure, and I never once wavered in my belief I was doing the right thing. True, I was moving right out of my comfort zone, and in the next day or so leaving my cute temporary apartment for a motor home I'd rented, and which was already on the site of Lavender Cottage. I had to laugh at the reaction of the girls when I told them about that. But I certainly wasn't going to be slumming it, I'd arranged for a top-of-the-range luxury American model complete with air conditioning, underfloor heating, and a good size working bathroom. Memories of drunken student weekends at festivals had convinced me I just wasn't a portaloo sort of a person. The motor home was a practical solution too because having been binging on *Grand Designs*, I'd seen for myself the advantage of being on site to keep a weather eye on things.

When I pulled onto the pebbled driveway of the cottage and stopped behind the magnificent shining beast that was to be my home for the foreseeable future, I think my mouth might have dropped open a little as a man emerged from a white van parked up nearby, holding out a hand.

"Ellie? I'm Chris."

As we shook hands, I was looking past him, still a little gobsmacked. "Wow, didn't know it was going to be *quite* this big."

He laughed, "You certainly have picked the crème de la crème. I'll just run through a few things with you, so you'll know how everything works." He handed me a full plastic folder, and smiled at my expression.

"Honestly, you don't need to read it all, it's pretty straightforward, and if you get stymied at any point, I've jotted down a couple of numbers on the front of the brochure, see? So you can call for help."

"Good to know," I said, "And trust me, I won't hold back."

I followed him up the steps as he opened the door and waved an arm, "Everything inside is powered by an on-board generator, or a mains hook-up. All mod cons, and you know about the underfloor heating and air-conditioning?"

"More interested in the heating than the air con right now," I said, "I feel the cold and we could have another Beast from the East with snow up to my ears."

He grinned. "Never say never, but honestly you're

looking at five-star here, you'll be toasty even if things do turn Arctic. You're not from round here, are you?"

"London."

He smiled. "Thought so, well, you should know it's not uncommon to get cut off round here. You don't need to worry about the heating, but best keep a full cupboard through the winter, just in case."

I nodded, mentally adding to my list which despite his reassurances already included the highest tog duvet available, and several hot water bottles for good measure. Meanwhile Chris was demonstrating the workings of the small but cleverly planned kitchen. It had everything I could need, even a washer/dryer, and dishwasher, and was so much more spacious than I'd expected. In the living area there was even a smart TV and surround sound.

"No neighbours nearby, so you don't have to worry about keeping the music down." I could see Chris's delight at how impressed I was. "Let me show you something else." He pressed a button on a control panel, and the side of the vehicle started to slowly slide outwards. "Gives you extra space, if you want to throw a party."

I laughed, "Wasn't planning to, but you never know."

"You're not going driving in it, are you?" he asked, and at my wry look continued, "Didn't think you were, so I won't load you down with information you don't need. I think we've covered everything else. Questions, or are you good?"

"Goodness, I think you've already answered all and any questions, so yes."

"I'll help you unload," he said, and I was grateful for

that; my cases seemed to weigh a ton, but by the time he'd followed my direction as to what went where, I was more than ready for him to go. I wanted to get myself settled, and look around the garden before the forecast rain set in. He hovered and I suspected wouldn't have said no to a coffee or something stronger had I offered. Action was needed, and taken. "Chris," I said, "Thank you so much, but I've taken enough of your time, and actually I do need to make some important calls now, so..." and I moved towards the door.

"Right, oh did I mention, pots and pans under there, you won't have to go out and buy anything in the way of equipment, and..." I interrupted him hastily.

"...And it was so thoughtful of you to leave me those numbers, any issues and I'll certainly call." As I shut the door behind him, I briefly leant against it and closed my eyes. It was all coming together according to plan, but I knew if I sat down now I wouldn't get up again, so I set up the kettle to boil with the lure of a coffee once I'd unpacked the essential groceries I'd brought. There was no doubt I was tired, but I could also feel the rising excitement. I was starting anew, wiping the thirty-year-old slate clean, pretty awesome. I knew the girls would want to see my temporary home, so I took some shots, posted to WhatsApp, reckoned I'd earned the coffee and sank down thankfully on the oh-so-comfortable sofa.

***

I slept surprisingly well that first night, something I never normally do in a new place and the following morning,

Ted the Builder arrived bright and early. I'd opted for him because he was also a highly skilled stonemason, had a good local reputation and worked with a team of tradesmen who'd been with him for many years. We'd met briefly a couple of weeks back, but this time he wanted to do a more detailed inspection.

He inclined his head at the Beast as I met him at the gate, "Well, you're going to be comfortable enough in there aren't you?"

I laughed. "Still getting used to all the gadgets and it's much bigger than I expected, but yes, slept like a log last night."

"Right," he said, "Best get down to things then." He started with the exterior, umming and ahhing softly under his breath and, I was delighted to see, taking detailed notes. He finished with a decisive nod. "Like I said, looks sound enough structurally, though some areas'll need attention, and that chimney'll need sweeping, jackdaws' nests, I reckon. Roof's not good. Leaks inside?" I nodded. "Hmm, and your windows are rotted, we'll replace like for like as much as possible, you have to have wood around here being the Moors National Park, but you can still have it double-glazed. If I were you, lass, I'd go for that, add on a bit to costs but save on heating in the long run." I nodded, and he made a note. "Right then, good news is your stonework's sound enough, let's see what's to do inside."

Tugging his earlobe – a habit I was to become familiar with over the next few weeks – he assessed what was going to be my living room. "S'pose you'll want to keep the grate, have a real fire?"

"Absolutely," I said, recalling the roaring flames from Hettie's time.

Lifting the tatty lino he nodded with satisfaction. "And it looks like we've got the original flagstone more or less intact underneath this. You want that restored?"

I nodded. "I'd like the wood panelling and beams renovated, not replaced, and I'd like the stone walls exposing."

"You've a good eye."

"Well I want to modernise without losing the 18th century character."

"Right you are, but you know you'll need a fair old bit done on your plumbing and rewiring. No gas pipes laid, so best to keep it all electric." He drew a card from his pocket. "Here, go see Bert, tell him I sent you, he's got the biggest showroom round these parts, kitchens, bathrooms, the lot, he'll see you right. I'll organise a skip so's we can get everything out that's coming out."

By the time we got upstairs, Ted had a good idea of what I wanted, and made some helpful suggestions on things that hadn't even occurred to me. When he left, I was exhausted but confident I'd made the right choice, and I could see he was genuinely looking forward to bringing the cottage into the 21st century. For my part I couldn't wait for him to start.

Trusty Ted was as good as his word, and the skip turned up the following day, the driver grumbling all the while about what little space he had in which to manoeuvre. In my oldest clothes, I spent until the early afternoon clearing as much as I could. The plan was to get as much done myself so when Ted started in a couple of weeks, he wouldn't have to waste his time with that. I moved slowly from room to room, taking care to prod shredded paper mounds cautiously before moving them, but the previous wildlife tenants seemed to have moved out. I knew the agent had brought in a specialist to deal with all that, but you never know, and I felt a lot easier once I'd swept away all evidence of prior occupation. I took the rusty old bed frames, hauled them – not easily – to the skip, pulled up the manky lino, dragged down the old curtains and rolled up the upstairs carpet, tying a scarf over my face to avoid inhaling fatal dust doses. The bathroom was all coming out anyway, but I took down an ancient Formica cabinet that had stayed up through the years attached only by faith and a couple of two very loose screws.

By that stage I felt I'd earned a break so I cleaned up a bit, and drove to the local deli in Whitby to stock up, such a lovely day. I parked up on the way home by Pannett Park. Sat in the park for a bit, and dropped into the museum, as I'd promised myself a visit. I was both fascinated and repelled at the same time by the Hand of Glory, but just had to sneak a look. The museum was ram-packed to the rafters with Victorian artefacts and curios. On my return I enjoyed a hearty ploughman's which wasn't really sure whether it was lunch or tea, but covered both satisfactorily. Following this with strawberries and Greek yoghurt, I showered and deciding I'd seen the best of the day, changed into my PJ's; after all I had only myself to please now. Chris hadn't been wrong about the efficiency of the heating and I had to admit the much smaller space was far cosier than my old spacious apartment. I put a soundtrack on the surround sound, and lit a Jo Malone candle, as it seemed to get dark far earlier here than in London. Closing the blinds, I settled down with a glass of crisp white wine, and a book, although I think I'd only read a page before the inevitable happened.

I was back at the cottage, alone, there was no other sign of life, and the chill and the dank smell indicated no-one had lived within the walls for a very long time indeed. I was floating aimlessly from room to room, I had to find something, and didn't know what. Confusion was compounded by urgency; I knew I had little time. As I passed an old mirror, I glanced at my reflection. Staring back was someone I almost didn't recognise. Dressed from top to toe in black, sweatshirt decorated with a heavily diamanté skull, shiny Doc Martens. My hair was shorter too, unevenly cropped, and dyed an unnatural shade of deep black. My shocked eyes met those of my reflection in a dead white ghost-like face. Heart racing, I moved on, and then into one of the bedrooms, where there was an urgent scratching from behind the wooden panelling. Something was trying to get out.

One of the panels was bulging, moving, strange shapes morphing in the wood. As if they knew where to go my fingers found an indentation in the panel and pushed inward. The panel swung outward. The scratching stopped. Something was watching? Listening? Waiting? The space revealed behind the panel wasn't large enough to be called a room, perhaps six foot high and the same across, just enough space for someone, or something, to hide or be hidden. An engraved wooden chest was on the floor in the corner, taking up much of the space and then, in the way of dreams, I was in the hidey hole too, looking down, understanding what it was that was trying to escape, and with a putrid gust followed by an impossible torrent of movement they did. Rats poured out, surging into the room beyond so it was carpeted in a foul, living, breathing, writhing nightmare. They were everywhere, climbing the walls, dropping from the ceiling. I couldn't move and then they were climbing up my body, into my hair, needle-like filthy claws piercing my skin, blood running down my face, my arms, my legs. But I couldn't run because this was what I'd been seeking, this was Hettie's hiding place. I reached for the box, but the lid slammed shut, and even as I tried desperately to force it open again I began to fall and everything went black.

CHAPTER 13

I awoke with a dreadful start, heart pounding, not sure as I slowly regained consciousness what was real and what wasn't. Of course it was only another nightmare, no more, no less. There was an intense itch on my leg, and as I reached down to scratch I shuddered, remembering. Rats had always been one of my greatest fears. I'd probably felt the irritating insect bite in my sleep and translated it to what scared me most, and my rolled-up pyjama leg revealed an ugly red lump on my calf. Trying hard to resist scratching, because that always made it worse, I rubbed in some antihistamine cream.

As I did that I had an abrupt moment of recollection, how could I have forgotten – in the dream there'd been a hiding place behind the panelling in the bedroom, an engraved wooden chest, an eerie glow, and then the rats. Ointment in place, I sat back. My logical side said, 'Calm down, dear, it was only a dream,' the rest of me muttered,

'But what if?' I rolled out of bed; with no work schedule to worry about, I wasn't even sure what day it was, but a glance at my phone told me and I was astonished to see it was after ten. I never slept past seven, must have been exhausted but a sense of urgency however misplaced pushed me on. I didn't even bother to shower, or grab my usual coffee. I was on a mission.

The cottage back bedroom, the smallest of the three rooms, was the one I'd chosen for myself, as the largest was to be converted into a bathroom, and the other would be a guest room. I felt it had a good, calm vibe, and loved that there was lots of light from the two small Georgian cross windows on the side wall, as well as from the much larger sash window which I lifted now, letting in fresh air and birdsong. The view across the garden to the river and forest in the distance was sublime. I was going to decorate with neutral colours, and had in mind a Victorian wrought iron bed, with a bedside table and wardrobe in stripped antique pine or light oak. But this wasn't the time for interior design planning. Turning on my heel I surveyed the wall opposite, where the Georgian painted panels which ran the length of the room were badly in need of renovation. I couldn't wait to get rid of the ugly dark green paint already peeling away in places and revealing natural wood beneath. In my dream one of those panels concealed the crawl space. It had to be on that wall because the other three sides of my room were solid Yorkshire stone. It didn't take long to inspect the panels, the room wasn't that big, but although I tapped and pressed every square inch, I could find nothing out of the ordinary.

Maybe it was one of the other bedrooms? But no, that just didn't feel right. But then again I was only going on the already fading memory of a dream and a gut feeling. I wasn't prepared to give up yet. I'd go over the damn wall again. This time I didn't only tap and press, I inserted my previously beautifully manicured, now much the worse for wear, fingernails into the fractional gaps between the panels. Even so, I nearly missed it, a tiny indentation at the side of a panel, and on the floor, unnoticeable unless you crouched down, a couple of curved marks where something had opened? I knew some of the older cottages in the area had been built with spaces similar to priests' hidey holes but here, near the coast where smuggling was rife, these were more often utilised for hiding contraband from suspicious customs officers. I'd missed the indentation on my first search because it was so ingrained with dirt. For a moment I wondered whether I'd been mistaken, maybe it was just a flaw in the wood, but then it gave under my fingers and the panel swung open.

As in my dream, the cramped space could hardly be called a room, there was barely space for me to climb in, and when I did I instantly felt trapped and claustrophobic. Thankfully there were no signs of my nightmare rats, and although it smelt musty, little sign of the water damage from the leaky roof which had stained the walls of the bedroom. A dustsheet was covering what turned out to be a mahogany trunk which took up a lot of what little space there was. Thankfully there was no ghostly glow, and of course I couldn't even be sure it had belonged to Hettie. I was shivering now, whether with cold or excitement I didn't know, but the sooner I got out of this space that felt as if it was closing in on me, the better.

Giving thanks for all that time spent in the gym, I dragged the trunk, which was unexpectedly heavy, out of the cottage and with a final effort up the steps to the motor home. I took a moment or two to get my breath back and grab a much needed glass of water before turning back to the trunk. It wasn't locked but was stiff from disuse, I broke a nail as I tried to prise it loose, and when it did give way, a damp musty blast hit me in the face; it had obviously been there for a very long time. It was filled to capacity, with a hessian sacking cover tucked over the contents for protection. I had the trunk on the spare bed, but now put a sheet down and started carefully removing items one by one.

The first few layers were bonnets, white pinafores, and hessian dresses, all pristine, and well laundered, and the care with which they had been stored touched my heart, as I laid them out side by side. Then there were three smaller wicker boxes; the first I opened was clearly the source of the smell, stuffed full of decayed fruit, nuts, mushrooms, and chestnuts. The second box held pine cones of all sizes, herbs tied with string, and brittle forked twigs. The last opened on locks of different coloured hair tied with thread, tiny birds' eggs, and several small hand-sewn cotton bags, which had held heather, lavender and rosemary, their scent lingering only a second in the air. Below the three baskets were stacked handmade flower presses, still preserving long dead blooms. And then there was another box full of watercolour paints, carbon pencils, and paint brushes, and a small wooden crate, stencilled Borough Market; did that mean London?

Inside that last box was a package which made me utter a small shriek; as I freed it of its wrappings I discovered a Hand of Glory, gnarled fingers black with age, but still recognisable, and missing a fingernail. I didn't know whether this was the one I'd seen before in the cottage, but I really didn't want to look at it any more than I had to, and swiftly rewrapped it. At the base of the trunk another hessian sack was protecting a string-tied parchment folder. Even before I untied it, I knew what it was, and indeed the very first sheet of paper was unmistakeably a portrait of Hettie, it was even signed by her. As I looked through other self-portraits, as well as pictures of Agnes and Bessie, I almost forgot to breathe. Bessie's mouth was stuffed full of blackberries in one, juice running down her chin to stain her white pinafore. A single moment in time captured so cleverly, by an artist with an instinctive touch. I couldn't believe I was actually handling Hettie's possessions, tears welled up both at the enormity of that, and the fact I was looking at snapshots of her life, fleeting moments of happiness and promise. I wondered what had become of Agnes and Bessie. I fervently hoped they'd escaped Hettie's fate, that they'd got away.

Pouring myself a glass of wine with a hand that shook a little, I composed myself so I could go through other seasonal pictures of woodlands, moors, studies of fruit, herbs, and flowers, my admiration growing; she was such an accomplished artist. I wondered if she knew just how good she was, and I was amazed at how little had changed in this area over the intervening years because it was still all so recognisable. And then I came across several portraits of an older man, dark hair obscuring his face; was this Hettie's lover, Bessie's father?

All over the bed were Hettie's possessions, and whilst I appreciated this was quite incredible, I had to admit a small part of me was disappointed. Had I perhaps expected something a little more mysterious than everyday items, something a little more magical, the knowledge she had promised me? It was clear the trunk had been packed with all that was precious in her life, ready for the swift escape she was never able to make. The responsible thing, I knew, would be to take the whole thing to the museum in Pannett Park, it would be of huge historic interest, especially the gory Hand of Glory, as the one they currently had on display was in a far worse condition than the one I'd just unearthed. Maybe passing everything along to the museum would help me get my life back on track so I could start living in the present, and leave my obsession with the past, back where it belonged.

The immediate task was to get rid of the smell, throw out the fruit and herbs, but as I started returning the other things to where I'd found them I saw there was yet another hessian lining with beneath it a slat of wood that seemed loose. With a knife from the kitchen, I gently prised it open and with little effort it came free revealing an extra compartment, in which there was a wrought iron tool with a looped handle and L-shaped, hammered flat hook, which looked as if it would be used to lever something up or open. The fact it had been so carefully concealed meant it had importance, but I'd practically stripped the whole house without coming across anything that the mysterious tool might fit, there was only the kitchen and storeroom left. I shook my head slowly. I seemed to be no nearer finding what I was looking for, and truth to tell I was rapidly running out of places to search, and with Ted due to start work next week, I needed to get on with the big clear-up.

Over the next few days, I worked like crazy, a woman possessed, stopping only for swift snacks, drink and sleep. As the skip became fuller, and my newfound DIY skills grew, I was exhausted but also enjoying myself. I'd never ever done anything like it before, always paying someone for any jobs that needed doing around the apartment, but there was no doubt I was now a whizz with the electric screwdriver, and could take a door off its hinges faster than I'd ever have thought possible. I felt an intense urge to go through the cottage again with a fine-tooth comb, finding every nook and cranny, and exploring every dark corner. Nevertheless I couldn't help giving a whoop of satisfaction as I lifted the last piece of tatty lino, and threw it into the skip. Kitchen cleared.

Just one room left now, probably the worst I had to tackle – I should probably have gone for it first. The room at the side of the house was where everything that wasn't needed elsewhere had ended up. It was crammed with all sorts and accessible through a door in the kitchen. I had great plans for this room, Ted was going to open up the doorway, and the fireplace so it would be an extension of the kitchen creating an open plan kitchen and dining area. I took a deep breath and plunged in.

I'd found out the last tenant had actually been born and brought up in the cottage, and then lived there with her own family, only leaving when she was taken into hospital, where she died aged ninety. The last few years at the cottage, she'd lived alone, and the shopkeeper in the nearby village had kindly made regular deliveries of food and wood; it was he who called the ambulance after discovering she'd fallen.

To give myself a bit more room to work in the cottage, I hauled a couple of the bulkier pieces of furniture outside, leaving them by the side of the skip. There was no way I could lift them into it on my own, although even with those out of the room, it looked no less packed – there had been some serious hoarding going on. Racks and shelves along the walls were stacked with magazines and newspapers, some dating back years, alongside lots of tins of food dating from God knows when. There was a multitude of pots, pans, cutlery and crockery and more teapots than you'd imagine would be needed in several lifetimes. Most of the items were in too bad a state to be made any use of. There were two or three rusty old tool boxes, the contents of which would be of no use to me, although I'd ask Ted if he could do anything with them before they met their final end in the skip.

The fact that the cottage hadn't been cleared before the sale had been reflected in the price, and was probably why it hadn't sold more quickly. But by the end of the day I'd made progress I could be proud of, and there only remained one wall of shelves to be done and several boxes on the floor. I was also pleased to see how much bigger the cottage looked without all the clutter. I could see a few boxes were full of vinyl LPs, which I planned to sort through the following day. Perhaps I'd get myself a record player, and I couldn't help grinning at the thought that I could play it as loud as I liked with no neighbours to complain. I put the records aside to take back to the motor home, and moved on to another box taped up securely; an involuntary 'yuk' escaped me, as it was full of what looked like sheep skulls, rabbit skeletons, tiny shrivelled mice and frogs, and deer antlers. Gruesome! There was a large manila envelope also in there and I removed and opened it gingerly, not sure what to expect. The envelope was full of grainy sepia photographs. Rigidly posed Victorian era adults, children, babies, and it suddenly struck me I'd seen similar before – in the museum – and I shivered. These were memento mori, I was looking at the dead.

It was the Victorian way of honouring, remembering, and preserving the memory of the dearly departed. In the faded shots small children, flower-draped, had their eyes closed. In another family group the mother had her eyes closed, and was surrounded by her children, and then there were young twins, one with closed eyes, the other with a glassy stare. Hands shaking, I returned them hastily to the envelope. I felt it was my duty to hand these over to the museum, but I certainly wasn't going to be looking at them again any time soon, they were spine-chillingly creepy, what on earth had been going on in the cottage over the years? I wasn't easily frightened, especially after my recent inexplicable experiences, so determinedly put the finds to the back of my mind for now, and as I looked around the room was delighted to see it was now more or less ready for Ted to do his stuff.

As I did a final sweep of the floor, a shaft of sunlight happened to come through the window, momentarily illuminating dust particles that seemed to be rising in a corner of the room; there must be a draught coming from under the floor. On closer inspection I could see one of the flagstones looked odd, larger and cleaner around the edges where it joined the other stones. Was it possible there was a hidden cellar? I picked up one of my screwdrivers then remembered the mystery tool from Hettie's trunk, and drew a sharp breath as it slotted perfectly into the gap. It was a highly effective lever and the heavy stone rose with astonishing ease. Shining the light from my phone into the black opening, I could see a wooden ladder leading down, and there was also the sound of running water. Naturally, I had no choice, and grabbing the powerful torch from my tool box, I descended cautiously, well aware of the damage time might have inflicted on the rungs of the ladder.

The sound had come from the bubbling spring running along a gulley at the edge of the large underground space which seemed to extend the width and length of the cottage. I assumed the spring must be the source of the cottage's water supply, it certainly accounted for the damp and cold, but this whole area would have provided excellent cool food storage. It didn't look as if it had been used, even as storage, for a long time, in fact it was quite likely more recent occupants had no idea it was there. There was evidence though of some use in the past. Recesses cut into the wall showed where candlewax had settled on rough stone ledges. It was right at the very farthest end of the cellar that I spotted something that made my heart skip a beat. A parcel, in one of the recesses. Disentangling it from accumulated and tangled webs of long-gone spiders, I found it was wrapped in a waxed paper which provided some water proofing. What looked like a leather boot lace was wound and knotted tightly around the wrapping.

In my heart was a hope I'd found what I'd been looking for, although my head said probably not. I was dying to unwrap it but was bearing in mind the ladder wasn't as sturdy as I'd have liked. I could see by the light of my torch that woodworm, damp, and sheer age hadn't done it any favours, and if I slipped and fell, I'd be in real trouble. So with the parcel uncomfortably cold against my skin where it was tucked down my sweatshirt, I climbed back up with a lot more caution than I'd climbed down and breathed a sigh of relief as I arrived safely back on the flagstones, using the lever to gently lower the stone back into its rightful place. It really was so cleverly disguised that had it not been for that random sunbeam, I might never have spotted it.

Back in the 21st-century warm cocoon of the motor home, I realised just how chilled I felt, and grabbed an extra sweater and some hot coffee before sitting down with the parcel on the table before me. I was both impatient and apprehensive as I untied the leather knots and peeled back the paper to reveal a leather-bound book in amazingly good condition; the waxed wrapping had certainly done its job. And I knew as soon as I laid hands on the leather cover of the book, this was what I'd been seeking, the missing link I'd been so certain I'd find. I took a few seconds to try to breathe normally because at this moment it felt as if my heart was doing double-time, and then I opened it.

There was no possible doubt this was Hettie's *Knowledge*, every page packed with symbols, illustrations, and explanations, most of which even though it was in old English and faded in places I could understand. She'd had faith in me. Faith I'd find this and know what to do, when the time was right. In a daze I placed the open book face down on the table; there was something I knew I needed to look for, and by thus opening the spine I was able to insert a couple of fingers, and careful not to tear the material, located a tiny wrapped package, as I'd known I would. It was a delicate necklace with a shaped metal symbol, and with equal certainty I knew it was for my own protection. I undid the dainty clasp and placed the chain around my neck, the intricate symbol nestling at the base of my throat as if it had always been there.

Hard to describe how I felt at that point – electrified, I suppose is the nearest I can get, more exhilarated than I could ever remember. The places I'd seen, the things I'd done, and my career achievements all paled into insignificance. I smiled to myself, despite it sounding like a corny movie title I knew without a shadow of a doubt it was time to Waken the Witch. I also knew once I'd taken that step there would be no turning back. I also now knew that the *Knowledge* was an intrinsic part of me, it was why I could open the book at any page and instantly read and understand with a strange feeling of familiarity what was written.

I realised there were bookmarks at various points of the book, perhaps those were of particular importance. I opened at one of the bookmarks, and as I made to set it to one side to read, saw it had been written on too, but in a completely different hand from the rest of the book – and in modern English. I shook my head; could someone else have found the book? And then a shiver ran up my spine as I realised what I hadn't seen immediately. The handwriting on the bookmark looked exactly like mine, the note was precisely as I would have written it.

CHAPTER 14

Shaken to the core by my discovery of both the book and of the notes, I decided there was little point in sitting and speculating. I needed to continue my clearing work at the cottage. Although I was pretty sure I'd found everything I was supposed to, it didn't hurt to double-check. Ted had delayed starting work for a day, so I had a welcome breathing space to get my head and house in order. I certainly didn't want him coming across anything 'odd'.

The first skip had been filled to the brim and beyond and had now been collected and replaced, and it was satisfying to know I'd done a good job although again it was a complete departure from my past life – I'd never been one to enjoy a good clear-out, but now clearly saw the restorative benefits.

I'd repacked the Victorian photographs, and the Hand of Glory without looking at either of them again, put them back on top of Hettie's clothing, and taken the trunk to the museum in Whitby. The curator had been beyond thrilled, exclaiming in delight as he handled each object carefully having first donned white gloves. He assured me I'd be able to see all the items on display before too long. His enthusiasm and delight at the Hand of Glory was in direct contrast to my own reaction. Apparently it was extremely rare to find one in such good condition. The gruesome hand already in their possession was on display, and with great ceremony he unlocked the glass case and with due care and attention installed his newest acquisition at the forefront, in pride of place, saying he'd deal with the labelling right away. I left with a sense of satisfaction that I'd at least made somebody very happy.

I needed to find a temporary hiding place for the book, and eventually secreted it behind some piles of crockery in one of the cupboards which stretched surprisingly far back in the van. It felt incongruous leaving it there, and the sooner it was back in the cottage where it belonged, the better I'd feel. I'd sent off for a sturdy art folder in which to store Hettie's paintings and drawings, and thought I might get some professionally framed to display on my newly decorated walls. I hadn't taken off the silver necklace since I'd put it on, as it made me feel closer to Hettie, and to my heritage. The most urgent matters dealt with, I turned attention to the boxes of vinyl LPs.

Along with the art folder, I'd ordered some boxes designed specifically for vinyl which was definitely making a comeback. Amongst the records were lots of old stuff that didn't really interest me, but I was delighted to find a Kate

Bush collection and made a mental note to buy myself a record player. For the time being I had to be satisfied with downloading and enjoying her magical voice, smiling as I listened to the dark lyrics of 'Waking the Witch' – she might have been talking directly to me. Delving further I found Siouxsie and The Banshees, and with song titles such as 'Spellbound' and 'Into the Light' wondered who'd originally made the purchases; there certainly seemed to be a focus on the darker side of 80s music. Coming across various groups I'd not heard of before, The Cult, Japan, Echo and the Bunnymen, I made up my mind to educate myself further on this other legacy from a previous inhabitant. With every day that passed I felt more and more that my decision to come here hadn't really been a choice – Lavender Cottage had chosen me. That didn't scare me, I genuinely felt I'd come home, convinced this was a mystical place where magic had been happening for a long, long time. I was experiencing a completely different lifestyle with no career in sight, yet I was feeling free as a bird. There wasn't a broomstick, black pointed hat or black cat in sight, but I'd quite accepted I was a witch in progress! I was thrilled at the thought of the knowledge now in my possession, and it was never a question of if, just where and when I would use it.

Brought back to the more mundane by Ted's knock on the door, I was pleased to see he was as cheerful as ever, shaking his head in admiration at just how quickly I'd filled the previous skip. He'd reckoned they wouldn't need a fresh one for another week, but I'd proved him wrong.

"Anything interesting, amongst all the rubbish?" he

said, as we walked over to the cottage, "Secret treasures, and the like?" We both laughed.

"Sadly not, but lots of boxes with stacks of records," and added, "But I did uncover a secret, a cellar."

He stopped in his tracks, "Did you, by 'eck," he said, "What's down there then?"

I laughed, "If you're thinking bottles of smuggled brandy you're going to be disappointed, there wasn't anything, other than fresh water running under the cottage."

He glanced around before continuing in a quieter voice, "You do know, there's always been talk of witches – not just one generation, mind. That's why the place didn't sell quickly, most locals give it a wide berth."

I feigned shock. "Lucky I'm not superstitious, I hadn't heard, but maybe you'll find something spooky when you start the renovation work."

He nodded, but he wasn't laughing "Aye, and hand it over quick as a blink, want nothing to do with anything like that." He paused as if considering whether to go on. "It's not all in the past though, you know, just you be sure to look after yourself. I'm not the only one's heard word of strange goings on. Nothing you can pin down, just the odd nod and a wink sometimes down the pub. Me, I like to keep a shut mouth and a deaf ear to any of that sort of talk." He gave himself a bit of a shake and reverted to his normal tone. "Now, lass, let's take a look at this cellar of yours, I'll need to check it out, 'specially if there's water running through."

Handing Ted the tool I'd found without going into

details as to where I'd found it, I stood back while, grim-faced, he lifted the access stone.

"You're not scared, are you?" I teased, and he laughed it off but I could see his mood had changed.

"Worked on a lot of these old cottages in my time," he said, as he put a cautious foot on the ladder, "This'll need replacing. Found some funny old things, that's all I'll say." I wasn't worried either on his behalf or mine, I knew he wasn't going to find anything concerning, in fact he wasn't down there long and I could tell he was relieved to replace the stone. "Best get you some electricity down there if you're going to use it."

"Maybe I'll have my own wine cellar," I said, and grinned, but he didn't. "That water's crystal clear, we could pipe it up for drinking water if you'd like?"

"Yes please, my own fresh water from my own fresh stream, I'd love that, now I'll get out of your way, Ted, I'm off to Whitby, might be back after you've gone."

He nodded. "Well I'll not be idle, you go on now."

We'd had some great weather recently and I'd been exploring the area, taking advantage of being near the sea, visiting nearby coves and pretty seaside towns. I loved walking or driving across the moors, solitude, scenery and a sense of being entirely at ease here. Autumn was creeping in now signposted by smoke curling from chimneys and trees changing from green to jewel-like reds, oranges and yellows. As I left the cottage and Ted's veiled hints behind me, I could see it was a far drearier day than I'd been used to, the sky dark grey and threatening. I resolved to stay in Whitby and not risk any moor walking first.

I wanted to visit Breeze Records, the retro store that bought and sold vinyl. I also thought that would be the perfect place to source a turntable, so I could actually start listening. I'd have a leisurely lunch at my favourite deli in Sanders Yard, although maybe sitting inside would be a sensible option today. I'd also decided it would be good to meet a few people my own age, but while there were noticeboards in some of the shops with details of local clubs and societies, I got the feeling they were more for the older generation. I thought though I might try some of the classes on offer. I knew there was Pilates, yoga, and tap dancing, and probably others, if I looked.

One of the big advantages of my new life was that getting ready to go out was far less of a hassle than when I was working. Nowadays I was happy with a smudge of lippy, and a dash of mascara. My health issues had also subsided, and were I hoped resolved, and my skin was back to normal, in fact I'd turned a rather flattering caramel in the sun, and my hair was in much better condition having lost its brittleness now the blonde highlights had grown out. I kept meaning to style it before I went out, but more often than not simply swept it up into a ponytail.

My first Whitby stop was Breeze Records. Within the boxes of vinyl I had discovered at the cottage, there were stacks I didn't want and still more to sort out. I reckoned as music was such a major aspect of life here and demand seemed to be going back to vinyl, Breeze might be interested. Glancing through the window I saw that unusually there weren't any customers in the shop. At other times I'd walked past it had been buzzing, which had always put me off going in, so this was an initial foray. Looking round with interest I saw it was retro decorated, and individual booths with turntables and headphones were set up so people could listen before making a decision. A man and a woman in their mid-twenties were behind the counter, both dressed in black from head to toe, which seemed to be the uniform around here.

"Can I help you?" The woman smiling at me was pretty with a smatter of freckles scattered over her nose. I smiled back.

"I hope so, I've recently moved into the area, and need a bit of advice."

"Well, welcome, hope you're settling in, and please ask away."

"Actually I'm renovating the cottage I've bought, and I came across several boxes of vinyl. I wondered . . ."

"Goodness yes, we're always interested and if it's not suitable for us we move it on to the local charity shops. I'm Lottie, by the way, this is my partner Luke, and of course we'd be happy to pay for anything we take." The attractive, sandy-haired man looked up from some paperwork, and gave me a small salute.

"Oh I don't want money for them," I said hastily. "I'm Ellie, by the way. You have an amazing shop, how long have you been here?"

"OK, we can argue about money if necessary, a bit later." Lottie laughed, "And glad you like it, we moved from Leeds a couple of years ago, so know what it feels like to be new, although my mum knew the area well when she was younger."

"I've come from London, so major culture shock, but I'm loving being near the moors and the coast."

Luke nodded agreement. "One of our main reasons for moving, Leeds was getting way too congested, we love the sea, and our flat's upstairs, so we couldn't be better placed."

"You certainly seem to be popular, you're jam-packed whenever I pass."

He smiled, "We've been lucky, younger crowd moving into the area, so massive music scene, they go for 80s Goth, pretty dark but they can't get enough of it. The Cure, The Cult, Siouxsie and the Banshees, and naturally Kate Bush – she's queen around here."

I laughed, "All my taste too, although didn't really listen to Kate Bush until I came here, but now I've started, I love her stuff."

"You'll have to come for one of our music nights," Lottie chimed in. "Some wine or beer and we settle down to some good old-school sounds."

"I'd like that, I'm just going through the records I seem to have inherited from previous owners, sorting what I'd like to keep, but you're so welcome to everything else. I'll let you know when I've gone through them and then perhaps you can pick them up, maybe next week? I'm in a motor home on the site."

"Well if you're sorted by then," said Lottie, "Monday's my day off, I can pop over, text me the address."

"Motor home?" Luke sounded envious.

"It's a pretty posh one, can't say I'm roughing it, although I can't wait to get into the cottage and spread out more. Which reminds me, the other reason I'm here – I'm after a music system with a turntable."

Luke made a small mock bow, and said, "You're in the right place, then." He came out from behind the counter, moving over to the display on the opposite side of the shop. "Something like this? It has a turntable, and may look low-tech, but it's actually packed full of all the latest sound enhancements, once you're in the cottage you can spread the speakers around the room. When d'you think it'll be finished?"

"Hopefully early spring." I made a crossed fingers gesture.

"So you'll be wintering in the motor home, that'll be fun!"

Lottie shushed him crossly. "Stop it, Luke, you'll put her off, although we certainly do get rough winters, roads cut off, that sort of thing."

"Not to worry, I've been warned, I'm taking no chances with food stocks, and I've been assured I'm severe-weatherproofed."

She laughed. "Well at least you'll have a good sound system, and a cool record collection if you get stuck in for a few days!"

"My thought exactly. When's your next music night?"

She reached under the counter and passed me a leaflet. "Next one's a week on Friday."

"Count me in," I said. "Look, I'm popping to Sanders Yard for lunch, but I'm taking your expert advice, Luke, I'll pay now and pick it up on my way home if that's OK?"

"No worries, I'll get it packed up now, even carry it to the car, when you're ready."

Smiling at having met such congenial company, I made my way over to the Sanders Yard deli. As I made myself comfortable on one of the saggy leather sofas inside, Melissa, one of the waitresses, recognised me and came over.

"Hi, Ellie, what can I get you? Some special specials on today!" I went for grilled haloumi with a Greek salad, and opened my laptop; with Melissa's recognition and welcome I was starting to feel like a local. I typed *myths and legends of the Yorkshire Moors* and googled. I was enthralled by the subject now, eager to find out more about the witches who'd apparently lived in the area. It made fascinating reading, and there were a number of contemporary articles I was working my way through. Theories put forward suggested practised magic had never left. It was sobering though to read reports of accidental and unexplained drownings of young women. It seemed that if the witches had never left, neither had the witch-haters.

The whole subject had become something of an obsession, and as is the way once online, one article and reference led to others, down a rabbit hole, until I became aware of someone's gaze and looked up. A youngish guy with long dark hair and tanned skin was making his way over to the sofa. I had no idea who he was, and his grin faded as he saw that.

"Will," he said. "The Ghost Tour, remember?"

It suddenly clicked. "Right, of course, I'm so sorry, it's just you look so different – no costume, no makeup!"

He laughed, "Yup a bit more normal today, certainly less spooky. It's Ellie, isn't it? But what about you, thought you were only here for the hen weekend?"

"Ah yes, well a lot's changed since then, I've actually

moved to one of the small villages on the edge of the moors, I'm renovating a cottage."

"That's a bit of a surprise." Then he added hastily, "Nice one though, but London to the moors, that's some change! Listen, I've just nipped in to grab a coffee and go, but how about joining me for a drink, tonight's my night off. I'll introduce you to a few of my friends, good for you to get to know some of the locals."

I paused for a moment before saying, "Sounds good."

"7 o'clock? The White Horse & Griffin, or the White Horse as we call it."

"The spooky pub we went to on the tour?"

"The very same, look, got to dash but look forward to seeing you later, I can introduce you to Tilly, my girlfriend, she's obsessed with London, so expect lots of questions." He saw me relax and grinned, understanding. I was definitely relieved, the last thing I needed right now was a relationship, not to mention he was too young and too Goth.

"London living is vastly overrated," I said "And usually by those who *don't* live there, but I don't mind lots of questions, look forward to seeing you later, and thanks."

He nodded and hurried off, and I returned to my haloumi reminding myself if I was to make a new life for myself here, perhaps in the future maybe I should be a little more open-minded about who was or was not 'my type'.

I took my time over a lovely lunch, relishing the fact I had no-one to answer to but myself, and afterwards dropped into the deli across the road to pick up a few things. Their fresh eggs came from a local farm, and I loved the artisan bread they stocked. I'd made up my mind to shop locally and avoid soulless supermarkets as much as I could. I also knew if I was going to continue wolfing down gorgeous baked goods with lashings of butter, I'd have to step up the exercise. As I put my shopping in the boot, Luke spotted me and moments later emerged from the shop with a large neatly wrapped box, depositing it carefully next to the shopping. I thanked him, waved at Lottie who was watching from the window, and drove home with a growing feeling of contentment. I was looking forward to setting up my brand new, stuffed with tech record player, and enjoying my records.

Ted had left for the day by the time I got back, and I had a quick tour around the cottage. I could already see evidence of the work he was doing and the skip was filling up again. On my way back to the motor home I cut some of the wild flowers from my garden; in a large jug, they looked gorgeous. Once inside I caught up on messaging the girls. I hadn't spoken to them as much as usual, and I missed them. I brought them up to date on the cottage, Lottie and Luke at Breeze Records, bumping into Will, and how I thought I was being asked out. I couldn't wait for them to see the cottage. I knew for a fact eco-warrior Alice would like it, but wondered what they'd all make of my metamorphosis from city slicker to country bumpkin. They were still worrying about my health but I assured them I couldn't feel better.

When I left later for the pub, the wind had whipped up and there was a distinct chill in the air, maybe a storm was brewing. I'd booked a cab so didn't have to worry about driving and was intrigued if a little nervous at meeting a whole bunch of new people. I was aware they wouldn't be the corporate types who used to form my social circle. I needn't have worried though, because it seemed everyone wanted to get to know the new girl, and Tilly proved Will right with her questions. Camden in particular appealed to her, as she loved Amy Winehouse, but she remained baffled as to how I'd been happy to leave all that for the wilds of Yorkshire. Will's friends turned out to be a great crowd, some originally from farther afield but most from different parts of Yorkshire. They all worked locally, farmers, teachers, others in local industry and services, and although some of them were quite a bit younger than me it didn't seem to be an issue. During the evening several others turned up, were introduced, had a swift drink and left, but our core group remained, and I was starting to put names to faces.

Unsurprisingly Will, a natural entertainer, was the lynchpin, recounting his latest ghostly experiences, combined with his client experiences on some of the tours. He was so good, I for one wasn't sure what was real and what wasn't, it all sounded equally convincing. Some of his stories weaved in and out through the centuries, and Tilly, who'd obviously heard it all before, rolled her eyes at me and we both laughed. I was enjoying myself, and felt surprisingly comfortable in a crowd of others who were obviously extremely comfortable with themselves and their lives. Someone had put a track on the juke box, Kate Bush's 'Waking the Witch', which made me smile as I relaxed back in my cushioned seat, near the fireplace – first fire of the season – and tuned in and out to the different threads of conversation. There was a real sense of happiness and simple pleasure in the evening, which was a contrast to time spent with my London set where there was always a slight undercurrent of rivalry about money, possessions, holidays and career ladders. Arriving back at the motor home later that night, I was pleased my head was still clear. One of the girls who lived nearby wasn't drinking, as she had to be up for work early, and offered to drop me home. I was warmed by the reception from Will and his friends, but peeling off my clothes, I could feel the chill in the air and bumped up the heating. Settling into bed, I put on a sleep podcast, and it didn't take long for it to work.

... I was in the motor home, but something wasn't quite right, I wasn't alone. A soft sound was coming from the spare bedroom; was I dreaming? No, definitely not. Equally definitely I knew I'd locked the door as I came in. What had got in despite that? What was making a sound like a cat mewing? I'm not ashamed to admit, it took me a long time to get out of bed to investigate, and the shiver as I did wasn't just from the chill of throwing off the duvet.

A young woman sat on the bed, head bowed, softly crying. In black sweatshirt, black skinny jeans, with short dark hair shaved on one side, punk like, I had no idea who she was as she looked up at me.

"Ellie, please help me." With a shock that ran from head to toe I realised it was Hettie. Gone was the long hessian dress and pinafore, her face was ghoulishly pale, and black makeup from heavily kohled eyes ran down her cheek with the tears.

"Hettie?" I said, "What are you doing here? What on earth are you wearing? How did you get in?"

She stopped crying, and looked baffled. "This is what I

always wear." I passed her a tissue so she could wipe her eyes. She seemed as confused as me. What the hell was going on?

"Can I stay here for a while?"

"Of course, but..."

"Thank you, thank you."

"Look," I said, sitting on the other end of the bed, "You should know I found the trunk, all your clothes, the book, and look." I leaned towards her as I pulled the necklace from the neck of my pyjamas, "The necklace you hid in the book's spine."

She backed away a little and shook her head, eyeing me cautiously.

"I'm really sorry, but I've no idea what you're talking about, what book?" Before I could reply, the motor home moved, and she looked petrified.

"Oh my God, they've found me, I have to hide." I looked around helplessly, the only place was the wardrobe. As she shifted the clothes and moved in behind them, the motor home moved again, first one way then the other, it was being rocked from either side. I lifted the blind; it was pitch black outside but as my eyes adjusted I could see we were surrounded by what seemed to be an angry mob, all men, all dressed in black. Unbelievably they were armed with rocks and first one then others drew back their arms and started throwing. The missiles were hitting the motor home hard; I expected one to come through the window any second, and backed away.

They were chanting, a low drone that increased in volume until individual words could be heard, the same words over and over. There was no doubting the strength of their aggression and their determination to get whoever was in here. I suddenly remembered there was an on-board security system in these motor homes, pressing the button on the control pad would send an alarm to the office manned 24/7, and it would be made more secure with shutters that came down automatically. We were now listing dangerously far to one side and then the other, and it was only a matter of time before they had it over. I flipped open the control panel lid but faced with two rows of buttons and several switches, couldn't think which was the one I so desperately needed, and with a huge bang and the crash of everything falling, the motor home finally surged over...

I woke with a start; the massive crash was real, the noise still going on. I remembered the men surrounding the motor home and Hettie hiding in the wardrobe. In a panic, still somewhere between awake and asleep, I hastily checked the wardrobe, but of course there was no-one there. Fumbling for my phone by the bedside, I saw it was 4am. The on-board security system had kicked in with the window screens down and in place, and nothing else had been disturbed, but what was that dreadful crack and crash? I opened the door carefully, only to have the wind nearly rip it from my hands. The rain was lashing down, and then there was another ear-splitting crack, as the sky lit up with a flash of lightning. I'd been sleeping through what must be the storm of the century. I withdrew hastily, locked the door again and returned to bed. I only hoped I'd sleep dreamlessly this time.

CHAPTER 15

Flaming June! I found it almost impossible to believe I'd been in Yorkshire for nine months, coming on for a year! The best decision I'd ever made, but where had the time gone? I'd loved every minute of it, but my concern, or at least one of my concerns at the beginning, had been the isolation, would I miss the London buzz? But nothing could have been further from the truth and looking back I realised I'd been far lonelier amongst my London crowd. I'd thought for so long that their values reflected mine, but it turned out they didn't at all. Maybe that explained that continuous slight sense of dislocation I'd felt, even when things seemed to be going well for me. Although my time here had gone swiftly, I'd crammed in a heck of a lot, and that's putting it mildly.

Alice, Sarah, and Lizzie had descended for a somewhat hysterical, and hugely enjoyable weekend stay. Work on the cottage was ongoing – a far bigger project than I thought, the budget had doubled – so we all squeezed into the motor home. I felt a little guilty I wasn't being completely straight with them, not lying, more a sin of omission. I hadn't told them about my continued time dislocations, not to mention the secrets the cottage had revealed. I knew they'd think I was stark raving mad and might move heaven and earth to persuade me back to the city. Taking them round the cottage, I offered a whitewashed version with which, knowing no better, they were perfectly happy. In fact, before she'd even got inside either the motor home or the cottage, Alice was enthusing, "Oh my God, the cottage will look incredible when the renovations are finished, and I love, love, love the motor home."

Lizzie had also been impressed with everything, but I knew she'd had her eye on me as much as on all the details of my new home, and once we were grouped on camping chairs outside the motor home, catching up with all the news and enjoying a glass of wine she said, "Ellie, you're shining! I know we all thought you were a bit bonkers, but you obviously made the right decision. I can't quite put my finger on it, but you've changed immensely."

Sarah added agreement, "Must be something magical in the Yorkshire water, this move was a life-saver for you wasn't it, I've never seen you so happy and content?"

I couldn't help a broad grin, they were so close to the truth yet still missing it by a mile.

"All my health niggles seem to have sorted themselves out, my skin, and hair have never felt so good." I dramatically flicked and pouted to prove the point. "And," I continued, "No more of those embarrassing fainting fits."

"You were overworked and overstressed," said Sarah, "that weekend when you had a chance to relax a bit, I think it all just caught up with you."

"And scared us all rigid!" added Alice.

"Isn't that what friends are for, to catch you whenever you fall?" I queried, then we laughed and the subject got changed.

***

I'd seen nothing of my parents since my last visit which hadn't gone well by any standards, and of course now I was a bit too far away for a short visit – for which I honestly wasn't sorry. I felt our relationship, already cool, had sunk to sub-zero after a particularly harrowing phone conversation with Sandy a few months ago. She'd turned into a broken record, going over the same ground, again and again.

"We simply can't understand, Ellie, why you've done this, dropped out of everything when you were doing so well. People would give anything for your amazing job and luxurious apartment. None of our friends can quite believe it either."

"Good to know I'm a subject for chats over coffee," I said sharply, "You know, it's not as if I've done anything wrong, as it happens I'm happier than I've been for a long time."

"Well, we think you're delusional, giving up everything you had to live out in the wilderness."

"Oh, Sandy, for God's sake I'm hardly trekking up the Amazon! Listen to yourself, no wait, listen to *me* for a change because I'm tired of knocking my head against a brick wall. If you and Geoff could be bothered to take up my invitation you'd see just how amazing it is here! But as always with you, it's your way or the highway."

I'd hit a nerve, and she instantly bit back, "How dare you, after all we've done for you, you're an ungrateful little bitch!" There was silence for a second or so, we'd crossed a line; we'd been near it before, but now it was well and truly breached. I felt wretched but kept my tone as calm as I could.

"I'm sorry I'm such a disappointment, but maybe your expectations have always been unattainable."

"That's as maybe but I'm afraid we're washing our hands of you. Go ahead, do your own thing, just don't come crying to us when you run out of money. I've done everything possible to protect you."

Strange thing to say? "That's not..." I started but she cut across me, "I cannot express how disappointed we are in you."

"On the contrary, I think you've expressed it very well. In fact you've made yourself exceptionally clear. I didn't expect your unconditional support, but I did expect a certain amount of civility." I felt my voice breaking, I had to get off the phone, but she beat me to even that satisfaction, hanging up first. The call brought me down, but I shoved it to the back of my mind. I couldn't live my life to please them, and I'd done nothing wrong, my conscience was clear. Just a niggling thought; what was she protecting me against?

***

My lovely Lavender Cottage had now been winter-proofed, so I was looking forward to a different experience this year, because even now approaching late summer the weather was turning. The motor home had been great, but nothing came close to living in an actual building which didn't sway back and forth when buffeted by bitter winds which always seemed so much sharper than those in London. I'd now been officially in residence in the cottage for just a few weeks, the novelty hadn't worn off yet, it was blissful, everything I'd hoped it would be, and more. With an efficient remote-controlled heating system, I could cope with whatever Yorkshire threw at me. The fireplace was restored and fully working, and I had a vintage pulley-operated clothes airer overhead, albeit more for appearance than substance, though handy nevertheless for small items. There was a small utility room off my kitchen, housing a washing machine, tumble dryer, and fridge/freezer, and lovely Ted and his team had used old scaffold boards for the worktop and the shelves attached to the stone wall. The electrician had also enjoyed using his creative skills with a galvanised steel conduit, hiding the electrical wiring, which gave the whole kitchen a wonderful retro look, as if it had always been there, ingenious! After an agonising time choosing the kitchen of my dreams, bringing the helpful chap at the kitchen showroom to the verge of a nervous breakdown, I'd opted for bespoke units which were sleek and modern, teamed with a reconditioned dark grey Aga; the mix of old and new meshed together perfectly and I loved the final effect. I'd even started experimenting a little with the

Aga cookery book. I'd be buying *Good Housekeeping* magazine next!

Every room in the house had been lovingly restored and furnished the way I'd visualised from the start – original features with a contemporary twist. The garden had yet to be landscaped, even though most of it would be ripped out eventually, and new planting established. I loved spending time outside, tidying it up as best I could. After an initial and possibly overenthusiastic attempt at rose bush pruning, when I managed to get an agonising sliver of wood in my eye and ended up in A&E, I decided perhaps the garden was best left to the garden maintenance experts, and I'd got them in to continue the tidy. I was probably better suited to sitting back and enjoying the fruits of their labour. We'd had an incredible summer and the garden bloomed bright so the cottage always had freshly cut flowers in vases. I particularly relished the lavender which grew abundantly, its scent constantly wafting in. I'd even gone so far as to order tiny hessian bags online, and filled them with dried lavender, placing them in my clothes cupboard and drawers, smiling to myself at following so closely in Hettie's footsteps. Now summer was at an end, I had to be more inventive, oven-drying orange slices on the Aga and collecting pinecones and tying them onto bundles of twigs to put in my vases, together with smaller vases dotted around with sprigs of flowering heathers and hardy cyclamen. I still hadn't come to a decision as to what I was going to do long-term, but luckily a healthy bank balance meant no pressure, so I didn't have to rush into anything. Of one thing I was certain, wild horses wouldn't drag me back to the corporate world.

I was fascinated by the rich history, myths and stories of Whitby and the Yorkshire Moors. And the deeper I delved the more I learnt, and the more I wanted to find out. So much so that I was toying with the idea of taking a history degree starting in October, going as far as finding out that there were last-minute places available. And I was also thinking about maybe following up on my other not yet fully formed plan of investing money in a local business, as there were always shops coming up for sale. For now, I was simply content to enjoy the beauty of my surroundings and my expanding social life, meeting people with no hidden agenda. Or so I thought!

***

With the move into the cottage, my disturbing dreams had almost completely ceased, and most nights I slept soundly and woke cheerfully, a contrast to the sluggishness that had plagued me in London. Neither had I had any more past life episodes, and it crossed my mind perhaps there was nothing else for me to find, no more life lessons to learn. Maybe I had all the knowledge I needed, or maybe it was simply that I was enjoying living in the present too much to let that slip.

As I said the dreams had stopped once I moved into the cottage but just before I did, whilst still in the motor home there was one which had a profound impact. It was probably triggered by my impatience for the move, along with my growing obsession with 80s music, and the alternative crowd I mixed with. I dreamt I'd returned to school. It was the early 1980s, I was in the sixth form, and I walked into a room in which there were six other students, my own age, four girls, and two boys. I was surprised to see them, in my dream I was certain I'd never seen them around before. They were self-consciously arty, theatrical types who'd obviously put a great deal of time and thought into their mix of New Romantic and Gothic. One of the girls particularly intrigued me; she had an almost ethereal beauty, and seemed familiar although I was sure we'd never met. I was disturbed because she emanated sorrow, heavy makeup failing to conceal sadness.

When I spoke to her she immediately turned away, but I wasn't to be put off.

"Don't think I've seen you around before, I'm Ellie."

"Oh, I've been here," she said, "I've always been here. Maybe you haven't looked hard enough." Before I could respond to such an odd remark, she started to move away from me. "We like to be on the periphery you know, keep a low profile, most people never see us." I shrugged; she'd obviously fully embraced a drama queen aura to match her makeup and clothes.

"I love your outfit," I said, determined not to give up, "You look beautiful."

She accepted the compliment as if it was her due. "It's my way of expressing myself, the only thing I have left. Everything else has been taken." I smiled uncertainly. This was a girl who wasn't going to bring sunshine into anyone's life, perhaps I was best off not pursuing any kind of friendship, but she still fascinated me. I took my phone out, and she seemed unsurprised at the cutting edge technology in my hand though even in my dream state I knew what I held didn't exist in the era I was in.

"Look, would you mind if I took a few pictures? It's for a photography project I'm doing."

"If you want," she said, without much interest, and obediently moved to different areas of the room so I could take a few shots. Her friends looked on expressionlessly. Together the small group gave out an arrogant and unapproachable vibe, as if they were sufficient unto themselves, and didn't need or welcome anyone else. I suddenly had an almost painful urge to fit in with them and for them to want me to fit in.

So intense was the dream that the moment I woke I checked my phone, but of course there wasn't anything there. I don't know what I'd expected, but unlike so many dreams which drift away like fog through your fingers, this stayed with me. Scrabbling about for notebook and pen, I sat up in bed, compelled to sketch image after image of the sullen Goth girl. Never have I been so glad of a talent I'd neglected since my days in advertising, sketching for the latest campaign. I managed to get a pretty good likeness.

Over the next few days I couldn't shake her off, she haunted me. Who was she, what was the significance of meeting her? She'd oozed understated Gothic cool, and I found myself eyeing my own wardrobe with a jaundiced eye. It was time, I felt, for bland country casuals to be kicked to the curb, they weren't really me anyway. I needed a new direction, I wanted to look like her. I know, weird, especially as I had no idea whether she was someone I'd met and forgotten, glimpsed in passing or simply created from my own often overworked imagination, but whichever it was she'd inspired me, and I knew what to do about that.

Armed with my sketchbook I headed into Whitby, to The Black Rose boutique. Lottie's friend Bella owned the shop, and I knew that having sailed through a fashion degree she'd used money from a family legacy to buy the shop and stock it in her own inimitable style. Some of the outfits she designed and made herself, others she adapted from vintage clothes. I'd gathered from Lottie that she was a quirky character and didn't hold back in speaking her mind, but I'd passed the shop many times, seen her window displays and knew this was where I needed to be.

Wind chimes sounded as I opened the door. The shop itself was tiny and crowded even with just a couple of people already there, one of whom was in deep conversation with Bella, but just as I thought I'd come back later, she looked up, caught my eye and smiled.

"You OK browsing for a few minutes?" I could hardly sneak off now, so smiled back and nodded. It was a fascinating place; despite limited space Bella had woven artistic talent into everything, pairing unlikely combinations to create unexpectedly effective outfits ranging from the demure to the daring. Going through the rails, I jumped as I felt something push against my leg. It was a beautiful jet black cat who looked at me critically with emerald eyes, swiftly assessed I had nothing to offer, and sauntered off with an affronted swish of a rather magnificent tail – probably one of the most effective brush-offs I'd ever had.

"Thanks for your patience." Bella turned to me as the others left.

"No problem, I could spend all day just browsing, you have some gorgeous things."

She acknowledged the compliment. "I'm Bella, how

can I help? Are you after anything in particular, is it for a special occasion?"

"No special occasion, just ready for a change, Lottie from Breeze Records told me about the shop, I'm Ellie."

"Ah," she said, and moved over to the door, switching the sign to closed and putting down the latch. "Any friend of Lottie's gets special attention." I must have looked a little baffled, because she laughed out loud. "Don't look so worried, it's just I always like to spend more time with anyone personally recommended. Hmm." She looked me up and down in similar fashion to the cat. "If you don't mind my saying so, my darling, you're dressed like a fifty-year-old, did you buy out Edinburgh Mill?" Direct *and* sarcastic, wow, Lottie hadn't been wrong.

I laughed, "Say what you think, why don't you?"

"I will," she said, "Safe, bland and twee!"

I liked this woman. "I take your point, look I've brought in a few sketches to show you the kind of look I'm after." She took the book from me, spending time looking at each one.

"You drew these?" she asked without looking up. I nodded. "Remarkable, you're a talented artist. Who's the girl?" I didn't want to recount my dream, this forthright woman would think I was mad,

"No idea, saw her in an old magazine. What do you think?"

"I think I've got some great suggestions, have you got time for a serious trying-on session?"

I grinned, "Well, I certainly know if I do, I'm going to get an honest unvarnished opinion, so yes, I'm in your hands."

"Great, but before we start..." She bustled through a side door next to one of the changing cubicles and returned in a matter of moments with a tray, gorgeously vintage china cups, a teapot, and two hefty slices of a delicious looking Victoria sponge. "... we simply cannot launch you into something entirely different without a bit of sustenance." As I accepted the tea and dug into the cake with enthusiasm, she spoke through her own mouthfuls. "The style is early Goth, not like the Goth look today." She indicated the drawings. "This was early 1980s, just before the floaty-sleeved, white-shirted New Romantics." She certainly knew her stuff, and as we finished our tea gave me a condensed but fascinating fashion history, which made me realise how little time or thought I'd spent on my clothes over the past year or so.

In the cramped changing room I tried on outfit after outfit, and Bella was tireless with a great eye and instinct for what worked and what didn't. We put together several day outfits and others for the evening. Every time I emerged she regarded me from all angles until she was sure, and in a couple of cases where she wasn't happy, she made short work of pinning until she was. She'd got the look spot on, exactly what I was after, sophisticated Gothic glamour, and on impulse I hugged her. "Thank you so much, just what I was after, I'll take everything."

She gave me a quick hug back. "Wish all my customers were such easy sales! You can take some today, and I'll do the alterations for next week."

Getting dressed, I was on a bit of a high, I couldn't believe how big a change the clothes made in me, and how perfect with my new hairstyle. I'd paid a visit to a newly opened hair salon earlier, where an eager young thing, couldn't have been more than nineteen, knew exactly what would work. She used jet black dye with a hint of red, then gave me a chin-length sleek bob, which swung gratifyingly when I moved my head. Naturally I'd had to change my makeup to suit the hair, and as a final touch in Bella's changing room I touched up my lipstick, a deep shade of maroon. In the same spirit of change and what-the-hell, I'd also had a tiny black rose tattooed on my wrist. The transformation had been completed with Bella's expert input. I was so moving to the dark side!

CHAPTER 16

Lottie didn't recognise me. When I walked into the shop she looked up, smiled, said, "Can I help you?" then did a double-take, and shrieked, "Holy shit, Ellie? You look amazing."

"Thank you, I've gone Posh Goth!"

"Bella?" she said, grinning.

"Bella indeed. I've acquired a whole new wardrobe!"

I'd got into the habit of dropping in whenever I passed the shop, or Lottie would pop into the cottage for a glass of wine or a coffee, depending on the time of day. As I grew to know them better it was obvious she and Luke adored each other, nevertheless they were sensible enough to appreciate working and living together meant it was healthier for each to do their own thing some of the time. Luke was always dashing off to scoop collections of vinyl from car boot sales or charity shops, or practising with his band where he played bass, and Lottie had her own busy social life. She was never short of visitors, friends appearing to view the shop as a local meeting hub, and several times over the months I'd arrived to find Lottie deep in conversation with someone. I couldn't help noticing they broke off when I came in. It wasn't anything I could really put my finger on, but it did make me feel a little uncomfortable, and I found it far more relaxing when she came over to me. I appreciated our friendship, I suppose she'd become my local bestie, and I felt we had a great connection, so maybe that slight discomfort and shut-out feeling was only in my imagination.

A few weeks after the great wardrobe revamp, Luke and his band were playing a Friday night gig in York, and Lottie and I had arranged to spend some time together. We'd talked about maybe going out for a few drinks but when I called her to finalise arrangements, she sounded pretty fed up.

"Would you mind if we just spend the evening at yours? Everyone's been doing my head in this week."

"You do sound tired, d'you want to skip it and get an early night?"

"You're a sweetie, but no, I'd love to see you, just can't be bothered to go out. I warn you though, I'm either going to be dead quiet or spend the evening venting."

I laughed. "No problem, you're welcome to bend my ear anytime, but I can do silence too, there's nothing else wrong, is there?"

"No, just a hefty whack of PMT."

"Well let's see if we can knock it on the head with some incredibly tasty stuff from the deli and a glass or two of wine."

Luke dropped her off once the shop had closed, and she waved not one but two bottles of our favourite New Zealand Sauvignon at me as she came up the path. In the cosy cottage surroundings, I could see her starting to relax a little, and between chatting and comfortable silences we'd got through a whole bottle between us before I bestirred myself to set out the cold goodies I'd bought. Lottie wasn't normally a heavy drinker, but tonight I realised she'd downed two glasses for every one of mine.

"Dig in," I said as I handed her a plate, "We need to soak up some of the booze." As she made a start, murmuring with delight because I'd remembered all her favourites, I went to change the record. I picked up 'The Hounds of Love' by Kate Bush, Lottie's mum had been a huge fan so she'd grown up with the music, and whilst I'd only recently discovered her, I'd grown to love it too; it seemed to be on everyone's playlist around here, they were obsessed with Kate Bush.

Turning over the record to side two – turning over being the only small drawback to vinyl – we sat quietly listening to 'And Dream of Sheep', 'Under Ice' then the third track in, Lottie came back to life. "It's so funny you chose this album tonight, this track says it all." I looked up. Lottie was slurring a little as she reached over to the music system and cranked the volume way higher. "Why do you say that?"

She laughed, "Waking the Witch."

I looked at her through the fog of too much wine. I'd cut down on my intake since leaving London and the unaccustomed alcohol was really hitting me.

"Yup, I love that one too."

Lottie suddenly covered her face with both hands. I wasn't sure whether she was laughing or crying. "You just don't get it, do you?" she said.

"Get what?"

"Do I *really* need to SPELL it out for you?"

I shrugged. I knew the wine had fogged my thinking, but I had no idea what she was on about. She sighed.

"Oh, Ellie, what the fuck, I can't keep it from you anymore. It might very well be the end of our friendship, but I have to be straight with you. I'm a witch. In fact, you could say I'm the Chief Witch around these parts."

I was shocked. I'd never heard her use the F word before, then I registered what she'd just said, took an ill-advised gulp of wine, choked on it, coughed a lot, and then started laughing.

"Well, that's not the reaction I expected." She peered at me, tilting her head to get me into better focus.

"Me too," I said, "Well I will be, at the moment I'm practising. No what I mean is I'm not a practising witch yet, but I am practising, to practise!" And I started to laugh again.

"I don't understand." She looked baffled.

I tried to untwist my tongue and start again, "I mean I'm practising..."

"No, I got that," she interrupted, "Of course I got that, you idiot, it's just that I *always* know, always see the signs, but *you*?" We gazed at each other, both of us slowed by wine and shock.

"Well," I said enunciating carefully, "I'm really a very

new one, d'you think you'd be able to give me the odd tip or two?"

She chuckled "Oh, honey, as if you even have to ask!"

From what I remember, and I'm sure there are bits I don't, the rest of that evening was incredible. Lottie firmly decreed there was to be no actual magic practised. It would be highly irresponsible, she declared, to even think about doing it drunk, and for some reason both of us found that so funny we laughed till we cried, rolling around on the sofa trying to get our breath back. We put 'Waking the Witch' on repeat, ditching the vinyl and using Bluetooth instead. Listening more carefully to the words, I was shocked to find out it was based on medieval witch trials. My head was spinning, I'm sure hers was too, I wasn't sure what was wine and what was incredulity. It was ages before we both calmed down enough to discuss things like sensible adults, helped along by a couple of cups of strong coffee each and some more to eat, and Lottie started talking.

Lottie had always known exactly what she was, but had few people with whom to share her version of the Knowledge. Her move from Leeds to Whitby, she said, felt like a breath of fresh air and the new start gave her the impetus and opportunity to finally nurture her talents and skills. One of the things she was particularly good at was seeing past the most ordinary of façades to pinpoint a witch, often in the most unexpected places and situations. Some of the women she approached were already well aware of who they were, others weren't, but Lottie maintained there were always signs and her witchy sense was usually spot on, which was why I'd thrown her so completely.

The majority of women to whom she made overtures were naturally initially suspicious and wary, and a couple firmly turned their backs – had no intention or urge to take things any further, but Lottie soon developed some genuine friendships. I could see why, she was authentic, knowledgeable, and above all she was patient, never putting pressure on anyone. The result of all this was that over the course of a year or so Lottie found herself at the centre of a small but growing community. If the witches of Whitby were eventually charmed by her, she in turn was stunned by the numbers of women cautiously operating under the radar, always aware and fearful of prying eyes. Before long, the women linking up with Lottie had evolved into a sort of self-help group – staying in touch incongruously on WhatsApp where they were The Mystical Ladies. Anyone reading their posts would have found them boringly banal and humdrum, and only those involved knew when an innocent conversation concealed someone in a tight spot, occasionally someone in real trouble and need, and in every case the newly formed sisterhood were there to help.

They met up monthly, always discreetly, with partners, friends, and family none the wiser. Ostensibly they were simply friends gathering for a night out although in fact it was invariably a night in – anything else would have been risky. At the same time as drinking in all this information, I was aware of Lottie's charisma and energy which was what had attracted me in the first place; she'd obviously exerted the same spell, albeit not in the magical sense, over the women as she was now doing over me. She was she told me scrupulous about who and how she approached anyone, although she still couldn't understand why she'd not spotted me. That evening was a revelation for both of us in our different ways.

The following few weeks were amazing, and I felt parts of my life that I'd never really known were missing, were slipping easily into place like lost jigsaw pieces. True to her word, Lottie worked me hard, an expert teacher with the patience of a saint, and because I was beginning to realise how much unknown, untapped knowledge lay within me it was a bit like riding a bike in the way it came to me. Lottie insisted I focus initially on just a couple of spells. It was important, she said, to do a few things well rather than many things not brilliantly, and when she felt I was ready Lottie announced she thought it was time I met the Mystical Ladies in person. I was excited but undeniably nervous.

"I'm only comfortable with one spell, they'll think I'm a fraud."

Lottie tutted, "Rubbish, everyone needs to start somewhere, you show great promise, just stop with the nerves. Each of us has strengths and weaknesses, it's those that make every one of us unique, you can't be good at everything." I wasn't convinced. "Reality check," she warned me, "Meetings can get quite chaotic, they're a sassy, opinionated lot, but not everyone's going to be focused on you all the time."

"Anyone special I should look out for?"

Lottie frowned. "I've only ever had a major problem with one woman. As you know we practise magic with integrity, for the good of others. There was someone who just wasn't on the same wavelength as the rest of us." She shrugged, shaking off a memory, "One thing you can rely on though, there's always someone to lend a hand if anything goes pear-shaped, as it often does."

"A relief to know they're not all perfect."

"I promise nobody's perfect, but the meetings give us a chance to learn from each other. You'll enjoy it."

When the evening finally came round I was torn equally between anxiety and exhilaration, and hoped the tingling running up and down my spine would be sorted by a glass of Dutch courage while I got ready. I had Lottie's support and backing, I just hoped I could pull it off. I was well aware that the special care I took with my outfit was defensive dressing, but we all need that some of the time. As if my first meeting wasn't nerve-wracking enough, Lavender Cottage was the venue for tonight's get-together, so on top of all the new-witch nerves I had hostess heebie-jeebies. I'd put on a long black pencil skirt, a firmly shoulder-padded blouse, and high-heeled shiny black patent granny shoes. My eyes were heavily kohled, my lips were my favourite deep purple, and as a final touch, I added an over-generous spray of Chanel. I'd chosen 'Night Porter' by Japan to lead my playlist, plumped cushions, set lit candles around the room, then for lack of anything else to do replenished my Dutch courage, and planted myself on the sofa to await the arrival of the Mystical Ladies.

CHAPTER 17

I suppose it wasn't surprising that I'd been stressing over my signature spell, designed to wow and woo the most discerning critics at my first meeting. I'd since gained quite a portfolio of so-called glamour spells and had been constantly practising on an endlessly patient Lottie. She'd suggested a beauty session for my turn at the meeting.

"No, that's an easy one," I said, "Not special enough."

She laughed, "That's daft." I shook my head. I wanted more of a challenge, wanted to make a spectacular entrance, show any sceptics what a newcomer from London could do. Seeking inspiration from Hettie's *Book of Knowledge*, something caught my eye and the more I read, the more I understood hidden clues within the text itself. Armed with this highly relevant information I decided what was to be my signature. I was determined to focus on the spell until it wasn't just good enough, it had to be perfect and I was delighted that when I did it for Lottie she'd been unstinting in her praise.

"Clever girl, I'd no idea you were this advanced."

"So, you think I'm there?"

"I'd say way beyond!"

I must have fallen into a light doze, maybe I'd overdone the Dutch courage, when I was woken by a knock. I just had time to throw a couple more logs on the fire before swinging the door wide. Lottie was first, followed by women of all shapes, sizes, and attire, some of whom I recognised, others I didn't. I suspected the big turnout might have been prompted by curiosity both to see the new witch on the block, at the same time as giving Lavender Cottage a once-over in light of its somewhat dubious history.

Before long the room was packed with astonishingly normal looking women, who might simply have been getting together for a book or knitting club. This was only compounded by the mundane way we kicked off with Lottie holding up her hands to quell the buzz of conversation.

"Ladies, please," she said as the excited chatter died down, "Firstly I'd like to thank Ellie, our newest member, for graciously hosting us tonight. We all know the history of this cottage, and I'm sure Ellie won't mind giving us a quick tour later." She looked over at me, and I took over.

"I'd be more than delighted, but don't get overexcited, even if we go slowly, it'll only take a few minutes." There was a murmur of polite laughter. "But I am very glad to welcome you here tonight." I only hoped they couldn't hear or see how nervous I was; this felt like a job interview but with added pressure.

Lottie took over again. "Right, any volunteers to take the minutes this month?" A stern looking middle-aged woman with long grey hair raised a hand to chuckles all round, and I got the impression she was the one who took them more often than not. She had that air about her, liked to be in control, so she might be the hardest nut to crack tonight. In her fifties, with tie-dyed t-shirt, and ankle-grazing skirt, she acknowledged the laughter as Lottie, said, "Ah, Susan my love, what would we do without you?"

"Now, ladies, we're quite a crowd tonight, so I suggest we split into break-out groups, that way we all get a chance to talk." She indicated the half-open door to the snug. "There's another room through here, so spread out, have a chat about what's been going on with you in the past month, then we can share some of the important issues." She paused for breath, then waved an arm at the food I'd set out on the kitchen counter. "As you can see, Ellie's conjured up some delicious goodies, although not magic, just the deli in Whitby. But..." she paused again and looked around the crowded room. Knowing her as I did, I thought *she's quelling any resistance before it even starts*. "Because we're so many, I have decided Ellie will be the only one practising this evening." This was as much of a surprise to me as it obviously was to everyone else. I felt eyes on me, not all of them friendly.

"Well, thank you, Lottie," I said, and if she caught any sarcasm, she didn't let on. "What a surprise! Ladies, I can only say I hope I don't disappoint."

Lottie, with a smile that brooked no opposition – easy to see how and why she was in charge – added, "I know you'll give Ellie the support she deserves, she's been working day and night on this complex spell."

By the time Lottie gave me the nod, everyone had talked, eaten, had several drinks and, I was hoping, was in a mellower mood. Women were squashed companionably on the sofas, perched on the arms, seated on the dining room chairs, or on beanbags on the floor, and all the other business of the meeting had been completed. Up till now it had all been noisily chaotic, but as I moved forward silence fell. I'd been able to assess during the evening that there were some pretty strong characters here tonight, and knew I couldn't afford to let my nerves show.

"Ladies, you are not going to like what I'm going to say next. I need you all standing up, please." There were a few groans, mainly from the bean-bag seated, but everybody did as I asked. "Thank you, now please join hands and form a circle around me." There were a few quizzical looks, and a couple of muttered comments I didn't catch but that was probably for the best. I clicked my fingers, and the electric lights went off, "Just modern technology," I commented, rewarded by a soft laugh or two.

As the candles burned brighter, shadows bounced on the walls reflecting the slightest movement. I closed my eyes, voiced my incantation and felt, as I knew they did, the unmistakable rise of energy from their joining hands and my muttered words, as I clicked my fingers for the first part of the spell.

It was as if time stood still, but I felt nothing happening. I opened my eyes in panic, fearing the spell wasn't working.

Closing them again, not wanting to see the satisfaction on the faces of those I'd already picked out as sceptics, I repeated the spell, making sure I voiced every single word correctly and at the right pace, and again clicked my fingers. There was a palpable shift we all felt and as I meticulously created the scene in my own mind, I was able to transfer it to theirs. I'd tried this several times with Lottie and even she'd been amazed at how realistic it was.

Visible first within the circle then slowly growing until it encompassed us all, was a forest, lit faintly by the moon above. Another finger-click and a host of tiny fireflies added their light. It was autumn, my favourite season, crisp bronze leaves carpeted the forest floor, and the scent of damp earth and moss blended with bark and those leaves still on the trees. I saw one of the women reach forward to touch the tree she was standing under, then smile as she realised her mistake. So realistic but so not real, and the next moment fawns came out to play, joined by squirrels and hedgehogs emerging from their hiding places, and as I clapped my hands twice, my *pièce de résistance*, fragile forest faeries.

They arrived in a group, delicate gossamer wings fluttering, translucent arms and feet emerging from rainbow-hued silk robes which shimmered in the fluctuating light from the fireflies. There was an audible gasp from the women around me.

"Forest faeries," I murmured, "From a time when these beautiful creatures lived free and undisturbed, deep in our forests." The joy of the tiny figures was unmistakeable, and I understood from the captivation of a room full of experienced witches, that I too was powerful. I added the hoot of an owl, the unnerving distant howling of a wolf, and the nearby sound of water free-flowing over rocks – OK, maybe I was showing off just a little. Across the room, I caught Lottie's eye and she smiled and shook her head slightly. I nodded in acknowledgement that enough was probably enough, and slowly began to let the illusion dissipate until all that was left was the very faint aroma of the forest at night, and as I clicked the lights back on, that faded too.

The room erupted in congratulations, with the best compliment from Susan, the minute-taker. I'd known she was going to be amongst the most cynical, hardest to win over but bending her head slightly she said,

"Bravo, Ellie, you have a powerful gift!" and the other women echoed that with a hearty round of applause.

CHAPTER 18

There was no doubt I'd brought the house down – literally – at my first Mystical Ladies meeting, and I'd even earned myself a standing ovation from the group. Although I still felt an element of imposter syndrome at our subsequent meetings, and had to keep pinching myself, telling my inner voice that I was truly a Witch. Lottie said this was to be expected, just a confidence thing, they believed in me, I'd won them over.

I'd earned respect from the group, surpassing their expectations, and quietening the naysayers who thought Lottie had acted too swiftly in bringing me in, but doubts had now been left at the door. I was grateful though to take a back seat at the next couple of meetings, and just watch magic from practitioners far more experienced than I. It had also been agreed that the atmosphere at Lavender Cottage was amazingly conducive and by a unanimous vote it had become the permanent venue for our monthly meetings.

Despite the confidence issues, I'd given myself a break, life was good, I was building some great relationships with many of my mystical friends, and I still saw Will and his crowd from time to time. I enjoyed the easy no-agenda friendship I found amongst them, and certainly felt welcome, especially with my new look. Naturally, none of them knew about my other circle, that was a door I was determined to keep very firmly shut.

I'd made big decisions over the last few months, signing up for the history degree course, and because I couldn't live off thin air opting for a different financial path. I was determined not to put myself back in the rat race, so was completing on the purchase of three, two-bedroom apartments in Whitby which I planned to let out to locals at an affordable price. I'd rented in the same complex when I first arrived in Yorkshire, so knew how well designed they were, and of course the big selling point was the view over the River Esk. Because the rest of the country hadn't caught up with how awesome Whitby was, I'd managed to get the three properties at a great price. I was going to bring them all up to luxury level, then hand them over to a letting company who knew what they were doing. I felt the hands-off approach would give me the time I wanted to socialise, study and practise magic!

I loved my current social life and the friends I'd made but it was seeing how hard Lottie and Luke had to work to make Breeze Records as successful as it was that had put me off my original idea of investing in a shop. In fact, the two of them were planning a much needed break. They'd hired a VW camper van and were taking off for Berlin to take advantage of the underground music scene there. Lottie's mum was coming to run the shop, I'd volunteered to help and was looking forward to meeting her.

But prior to that my girls were descending for a few days; this would be their first time in the cottage, and after boring them silly with all the details along the way, I was anxious for them to see the final result. We were regulars on WhatsApp, but there was a lot I hadn't disclosed, although to their delight I'd sent several shots of me in my new outfits. I trusted them completely, and over the years we'd shared most things, so I wasn't sure what was holding me back in telling them my biggest news; after all we all had skeletons in our individual cupboards. There was Alice's abortion, while we were at uni. A stomach upset had meant the pill let her down, and a one-night stand had consequences. She was devastated, but knew she wouldn't go ahead with the pregnancy, she didn't even tell her parents, but we were there to see her through it, and it was never necessary to mention it again.

Lizzie around the same time had started experimenting with what she said was harmless stuff, until we all began to see a change in her behaviour. We didn't know that much about addiction, but enough to recognise when things weren't right. She didn't appreciate our intervention one little bit, and was livid at the suggestion there was a problem. Nevertheless, we mounted a 'stay with Lizzie' programme, so one of us was always with her. She ranted and raved at us for a short time, but thankfully we'd stopped her in time, and she never went down that road again.

When we left university, we lost touch with Sarah for a while, and she just seemed to drop off the radar. It transpired she'd been seeing the father of one of her friends, and when it came out as these things tend to do, not only did the friend swiftly become an ex-friend, but word spread instantly through the village community where she'd been born and brought up, and things became very unpleasant indeed. By the time she finally told us what had been going on, the relationship had fizzled out, she'd relocated and was starting completely afresh. I too had had my own share of confessions to make through the years, but each of us had always been certain the others had her back. Which is why I'd finally decided to let them into my secret, and even demonstrate, perhaps a watered-down version of glamour magic.

The cottage was now sparkly clean, and ready for visitors. My marvellous, magical cleaner Cynthia had blitzed the place. Cynthia had a brilliant team working for her in her successful cleaning agency, but I was lucky that she saw to me herself. As she was one of the Mystical Ladies, she got the job done in the time it took her to click her fingers, something she would never risk doing for a normal client. One of the advantages of that was we always had time for tea and a chat.

"You know," she said, stirring her tea slowly, "Since you came on the scene, there's been a definite change in atmosphere," she paused for a moment, "more dynamic I'd say, like a breath of fresh air." I raised an eyebrow and helped myself to another chocolate biscuit.

"Mmm," she said, reaching for the plate too. "These are delicious, from the deli? Thought so. Yes, I would say overall the group seems to have lightened up, I know everyone was surprised at how powerful you were – for a newbie!"

"But they aren't hostile?" I queried.

She shook her head. "No, well just a couple of snide remarks from the women you'd have expected to make them, but no, the general feeling's really positive."

I was relieved. "I have been getting good feedback, but worried it might not be genuine, I was concerned I'd gone too far with my presentation, showing off a little maybe?" She sighed. "Don't worry, and don't forget, most of us have been around the block a few times, seen both strange and spectacular things in our time. Apart from which," she gave me a considered look, "I'm pretty sure if there's a problem with anyone, you won't hesitate to put them in their place. You don't seem very backward in coming forward." She got up and put on her jacket, a cheery number in bright red. "I must get going, thanks for the tea, and I'm going to stop off later and get some of those gorgeous biscuits for myself." She gave me a brisk hug and I watched her walk to her car. I knew she was in her early sixties, but she'd asked me to keep that to myself, everyone thought she was in her late forties, and she'd never bothered to correct them.

As usual Alice was the first of the girls to arrive. The cottage had been a building site on her last visit. As she came in, I noticed her case was much smaller than I'd have expected; Alice never used to travel light, so things had changed. Putting it down she gave me an uncharacteristic hug, then held me at arm's length to take a good look.

"Ellie my love, you look amazingly, beautifully Goth. And don't tell me that's a tattoo?"

I laughed nervously, relieved despite myself. Alice didn't hesitate to speak her mind and if she thought I looked ridiculous would have had no qualms in saying so.

"Life here suits me. Lots to tell you but not till the others arrive. Vino?"

"You bet, it was a long drive."

"OK, why don't you freshen up and I'll have it ready, and I've got lots of vegan nibbles, the ones you liked last time. I've put you in the back bedroom with me."

She grinned, grabbed her case and headed up the stairs. "Great, I'll be right down. We're going to have a fab few days, right?"

"Right."

Alice had only recently gone vegan, and I'd made sure she was going to be well catered for. I also guessed from the size of her case that she might have renounced her fashion fixes too, she'd really taken on board saving the planet. Back downstairs ten minutes later she looked, as always, simple but oh so classy. Handing her a glass of wine, I nodded approvingly.

"From Sarah?"

She sank down on the sofa with a sigh of pleasure and nodded. "She sources vegan ethical fabric, then designs and makes up for me."

By the time Lizzie and Sarah turned up, Alice had already had her tour, which I repeated for the others after we'd put their cases in the front bedroom. When they joined us downstairs, still enthusing about what I'd done with the place, it was Lizzie's turn to give me the once over.

"You look even better than last time we were here," she paused and looked closer, "Have you had some sneaky work done?"

I shook my head. "No way, it's all down to a wonderful beautician, Emma, in Whitby, I'll introduce you." I didn't add she was another of the Mystical Ladies. She worked her own brand of beauty spells, although not on her regular customers, that would have been too much of a risk. Sarah meanwhile had been assessing my outfit with a professional eye.

"Lovely," she murmured. "Well, I know we all thought you were mad, but this move has done you the world of good, and now your clothes have finally caught up – the country casuals look was never really you, was it?"

I laughed, "No comment, come on, let's eat." And laughing, talking, and relishing the best offerings from the deli, we spent the rest of the evening catching up on news, although at that point I didn't bring up the most important of mine.

The weather was kind, so we were able to enjoy the garden which had been a jungle when they last visited but was now looking completely lush and presenting a much better view of the brook, the unruly ferns now tamed. They loved the fact that it was so secluded, with the sound of the river in the background, and forest land as far as the eye could see. I told them I didn't venture outside of the garden, because it was so easy to become disorientated and lost, although the truth was, I avoided it like the plague. I'd never been able to shake off the shiver-inducing vision of Hettie's drowning. I'd let them do their own exploring.

We crammed a lot into a hectic few days, returning to the coastal villages we'd loved so much on our first visit, and driving across the moors again. We travelled further afield, to the market town of Helmsley with its Cotswolds-like cottages, lunched at the Secret Café at Falling Foss, enjoying its spectacular waterfall and the challenging walk leading to the Pennine Way. Alice was particularly thrilled that even a small café along the way had a vegan option, and even more delighted to find it was delicious for a change.

As always, their visits were far too short, the days whizzed by, and it wasn't until we were chilling out at the cottage on the last afternoon that I decided to broach the subject on my mind, as the timing felt right.

"Actually I do have a bit of news I haven't shared yet." Lizzie had been sorting through some of my vinyl, and Sarah and Alice were both scrolling through their phones on the sofa.

I paused for effect. "I've been practising what they call glamour magic."

Alice laughed, "Yes, well we can see that, although that brilliant beautician might have had a hand in things too."

"No, I mean..." I paused again, but it was now or never. "I mean actual magic."

Sarah frowned. "You mean children's parties, that sort of thing, that's not really you, is it?" Lizzie grinned, "Don't you always say, steer clear of children?"

"You're not listening to what I'm saying." Something about my tone of voice changed the jokey atmosphere in the room, and for a moment there was silence before Lizzie suddenly stood up, and gathered up some empty plates from the coffee table.

"I'll get these washed up," she said, and over her shoulder, "You know you really shouldn't joke about that sort of thing."

"I'm not joking," I said.

Sarah shook her head. "Oh, Ellie, stop it. This isn't funny."

And from the kitchen Lizzie added, "It's this cottage, you've spent too much time alone here, goodness knows what you and your imagination have cooked up. And..." she held up an empty wine bottle she was about to put into the recycling bin, "I think maybe you've had enough of this for today." The others smirked, then stopped when I didn't join in.

Lizzie, moved away from the sink, drying her hands. "OK, I'll play along, turn Sarah into a toad." Sarah looked genuinely alarmed, and this time it was my turn to laugh.

"It's exactly that sort of thing that gives witches a bad name."

"Witches?" said Lizzie, "Is that what you think you are?" I could see she was torn between amusement and losing her temper at a joke she saw going on too long.

I took a deep breath. "I expect you've heard of White Witches whose spells are benign, used only to help, never hurt." Lizzie and Sarah exchanged a look.

Alice said, "So are you telling us that you think you're one of those – a White Witch? Is that what you're saying?

Come on, Ellie, where's all this suddenly come from?" Then suddenly suspicious, she said, "Has somebody been... I don't know... influencing you?"

"No," I said firmly, "Well at least not someone, more like something. It's to do with where I am." I moved my hand to indicate. "It's the cottage."

Sarah shivered. "I don't like this, I don't like all this silly talk, can you just stop it, Ellie, it's freaking me out." I could see she was genuinely spooked, not just at what I was saying but by the fear I might actually be delusional.

"I promise there's nothing to be afraid of," I said. "Do you honestly think I'd tell you something that would put you at risk? But you have to swear this is something that won't go beyond this room." We'd made the same solemn promise several times over the years on different occasions, and always with the confidence that trust wouldn't be broken. Lizzie was the first to respond.

"Cross my heart, and hope to die," the phrase repeated by Sarah, and Alice who continued, "Come on then, if you've got something to show us, show us!" Alice's tone was a little sharp, it was definitely challenging.

"Right. Lizzie," I said, as she looked startled, "How d'you feel about a change of hair colour?"

Lizzie's face reflected uncertainty mixed with disbelief. "OK," I said, "everyone into a circle." I closed my eyes as one by one they joined me seated on the floor. The cynicism in the room was palpable, and as I muttered the incantation under my breath there were a couple of muffled giggles until I clicked my fingers, and there was sudden silence as blonde became a warm chocolate colour. Lizzie raised her hand to her head, her expression mirroring that on the faces of Alice and Sarah.

"She's done it, hasn't she?" Lizzie had risen and was already halfway up the stairs on her way to a mirror as Sarah said,

"It's some kind of trick isn't it? Come on, Ellie, you've had your fun, how did you do it?"

I shook my head. "Sorry, trade secret." Lizzie was coming back downstairs, I murmured a few words under my breath, and in the time it took to move from one step to another, her hair turned deep magenta. Again reacting to the other two, Lizzie switched directions and raced back up again.

"Change it back, Ellie," she yelled. I smiled and did as she asked then turned to the others.

"Who's next?" I asked.

Sarah was cautious. "Depends on what you're going to do." I looked at her; she was very much into the natural look, wore minimal makeup and wouldn't have touched Botox with a barge pole.

"What do you fancy?" I asked.

"Well, I could do with losing a few years."

"Couldn't we all," said Lizzie, now seated again; we all laughed, and thankfully that broke the tension which had built up.

Sarah continued, "Five years off, or maybe make that ten, I'd just love to get rid of the wretched crow's feet round my eyes?" I nodded, a straightforward enough request, although I did wonder for a moment whether this would be classed as a past spell. At a recent magical meeting we'd been warned against trying to make any changes to the past, but this was just a glamour spell, an enhancement of appearance, it really shouldn't be a problem, besides which I could always reverse it.

Eyes closed to aid concentration, I whispered the spell softly under my breath, and before I'd reopened them, Sarah had rushed off to the mirror.

"Ooh, everything looks so much smoother," she said as she came back down slowly. "All those wretched little lines have gone, but..." she was looking at her arm, "That's weird, my tattoo's gone." Then her hand went to her mouth, and she gasped, "*And* all my expensive dental work, Ellie, I spent a fortune on straightening and whitening." Sarah had this thing about her teeth, in fact it was her only cosmetic concession.

"Relax," I said, "I can easily reverse the spell, if that's what you want?"

She took a moment to think. "Well, I love the face, but I paid a fortune for the teeth, and the tattoo has special meaning for me, so I suppose yes, that's what I want." Reversing was always quicker, and we watched as before our eyes Sarah subtly aged the few years I'd taken away.

"Alice?" I said, "Fancy a go?" After the initial revelation she'd gone quiet, just watching and listening. I could see she felt uneasy.

"Don't look so worried," I said, "Of course you don't have to do anything you don't want to."

She shook her head. "To be honest, Ellie, I'm absolutely fascinated, and if I hadn't seen it with my own eyes I'd never have believed it, but it's far more important to talk about what you're getting yourself into here, I'm really worried."

I started to say that I was only working at a very low level, but she spoke over me. "I'm scared for you, Ellie, this is so way beyond normal experience."

"Alice, I promise you, you have my word, I'm not going to do anything silly. And I quite understand you don't want to experiment." I rose to my feet. "I'll get supper going."

"No," she interrupted, "Freckles."

"Freckles?"

"Yes, I hate them, always have. Can you get rid of them?"

"Really?"

"In for a penny in for a pound," she said.

"I haven't done this one before so..."

She interrupted again, "Ellie, just get on with it before I change my mind, what can go wrong?"

We formed the circle, but before I'd even completed the spell there were gasps from Sarah and Lizzie, and opening my eyes I was horrified. Instead of ridding Alice of the hated freckles, I appeared to have made them ten times worse. They were now covering the whole of Alice's beautiful face. Seeing our reaction, she started to panic. I rushed after her as she dashed up the stairs but not in time to stop her shriek of despair as she saw her reflection. By then, I'd realised what had happened, I'd used the formula the wrong way.

"Alice, I can sort it, please don't worry."

"Look what you've done!" she yelled, then sat suddenly

on the bed, and started to sob, her usual ice queen cool shot to pieces. I couldn't ever remember seeing her in such a state before.

"This is my very worst nightmare," she moaned. "I must have been completely mad to let you try."

"I can reverse it," I said, "Honestly, calm down." We rarely fell out, but now she stood up and screamed in my face,

"I don't want your excuses, just bloody well sort it out." I closed my eyes and, focusing totally on what I was doing, repeated the spell, with the vital part the right way this time. Then I took a deep breath and opened my eyes. Thank God, every single freckle on her lovely face had disappeared. I put both hands on her shoulders and turned her to face the mirror. There was a pause while she took in her appearance, turning her face this way and that.

"You do realise I would have sued you?" she said solemnly, then seeing the look on my face, "Don't be daft, I'm not serious, I don't think witchcraft is recognised by the law these days."

CHAPTER 19

On the last morning of their visit we enjoyed a long lazy continental breakfast, churned butter, and eggs from the local farm shop and strawberry jam, crusty bread, croissants, and pastries from my favourite deli. I'd made a rich creamy porridge, adding fruit and syrup to the mix, plus gallons of strong black coffee, and a carafe of fresh orange juice with extra juicy bits.

I'd finished last night's little display by sorting Sarah, back had come the teeth and the tattoo, but to her delight after experimenting I'd managed to eliminate the despised crow's feet. As we sat ourselves round the kitchen table there was a slight air of constraint and a short silence while everyone helped themselves to breakfast. I could see that each in their own way was processing what had happened. I knew the silence would be short-lived.

Lizzie was the first to open fire, asking about her chocolate truffle hair that after some experimentation she had finally decided on. I explained that as it was a spell it wouldn't grow out, and could see her calculating time and money saved at the hair salon, but framed by her new hair she was frowning now.

"How on *earth* did this all happen, how did you find out how to do all this?" She waved an arm, taking in the changes I'd wrought in all of them. I chose to ignore the question.

"Just let me know when you want a colour change, I can do the whole spectrum," I said.

Sarah plunged in next. 'Come on, Ellie, seriously, where did all this come from, are there other witches around here?" She was getting too near the truth, and with a laugh, I tried to head her off.

"Told you before, if I tell you I'll have to kill you."

She shrugged. "Might well be worth it, I'm dying to know." Of the three, Alice was the one who seemed to have taken things most in her stride.

"Well, I'm just grateful," she said, "Love the no-freckles look." I was surprised she wasn't bursting with curiosity like the other two, but knowing she was like a dog with a bone when she was determined to get to the bottom of something, I was just grateful. Although it was odd, because she was the most feet-on-the-ground of all of us.

I was sad to say goodbye to them, but glad to catch up on sleep after all the late nights. I knew I had to be fighting fit for my week at Breeze, helping out Lottie's mum.

Dressed to impress for comfort and style, black leather pencil skirt, black chiffon blouse, black tights and granny shoes, my makeup and hair pure 80's Goth, I set out in good time the following Monday, to report for duty. I was looking forward to meeting my temporary workmate; apparently she and Lottie were more like sisters than mother and daughter, and that had made me smile wryly when Lottie told me, as it was a relationship I could never envisage with my own mother. As we introduced ourselves and I took in her only slightly tamer version of Siouxsie Sioux's hairstyle, dark kohled eyes and bright red lipstick setting off her olive skin, I chuckled to myself again. She couldn't be further removed in appearance from my extremely conservative mother, if she tried.

She'd been concentrating on sorting vinyl when I got there, but when she looked up and smiled, I could immediately see Lottie in her. Her flatteringly low-cut top shifted as she reached to put records on shelves and turned to me, but just before she straightened it I glimpsed a tiny heart-shaped mole, which looked just like mine, and in a similar place too; how funny. I meant to mention it to her but got sidetracked finding out how everything had gone the previous week.

"I'm so sorry I wasn't able to help out, I had friends staying."

She smiled, "No problem at all, it was fine actually, no huge rushes, just nice and steady. Now, kettle's just boiled – tea or coffee?"

"Coffee please, splash of milk, no sugar," I said, taking off my jacket and hanging it up. As we perched on a couple of stools savouring our drinks, she grinned.

"First thing's always quiet, we've usually got until 11.00 before we get busy, so this is an opportunity to find out more about Lottie's new best friend."

Our early morning coffee and chat became a daily occurrence, and as the week went on, we found out more about each other. Anna had lived in the area as a teenager.

"Bit of a tearaway," she said, "Never could stand boring."

"Well you haven't changed, have you," I laughed, nodding at the hair and makeup. "Boring you certainly are not." I was delighted she and I had so quickly reached the stage of being able to gently tease each other – with some people that never happened. She'd also earned my affection by stopping daily at the deli for a treat or two to have with our coffee. She'd heard from Lottie that I'd moved from London and demanded the whole story.

"It all started with a hen party," I told her. "I thought they'd all love the Goth weekend, and in the few days we were here I fell in love with the place." I paused to reach for another of the small almond biscuits she'd opted for that morning. "So long story short, I left my job, sold my apartment, and bought and renovated a wreck of an 18th-century cottage."

"You don't believe in hanging around, do you?"

"Suppose not, but actually it just seemed the right thing to do."

"Any regrets?"

I shook my head. "No, it's been a complete and utter change, but I love it and the local boutiques have proved perfect for my style."

She looked me up and down approvingly. "Just how I used to dress in the 80s."

"I'll take that as a compliment," I said, and got up to serve a customer who'd just come in.

Anna was fun, efficient to work with, and good company; our age difference didn't seem to come into it, and we worked side by side between customers, sorting vinyl, and listening to different tracks as we went along. I thought I was really up on 80s music, but Anna's knowledge was phenomenal, and what she didn't know, wasn't worth knowing. The only minor downside was that I ended up spending a fortune on new vinyl. The week had got steadily busier as it went on, with an influx of holidaymakers, as well as loyal locals who had all decided, it seemed, to increase their vinyl collections. At the same time we sold some pretty expensive turntables, speakers, and a variety of other music-lovers' accessories. Luke was going to have to restock. Thankfully though by the Friday, the penultimate day of my stint, things seemed to have slowed down a little, and I insisted on going to the deli to get lunch, my treat.

As we tucked in, Anna said, "I haven't asked how your renovations are going. I'm in a modern house now, but did a renovation project a few years ago so know all the headaches involved."

"Actually I think I was pretty lucky, I used a great local firm, it's all done now, in fact if you're not busy, why not come over tonight and have some supper with me, then you can see for yourself?"

She smiled and nodded. "Well, if you're sure it won't be a bother, I'd love to. Whereabouts are you exactly?"

"Just outside Eastcombe, d'you know it? If you just drive straight through, Lavender Cottage is down the road." I was cutting myself another piece of the delicious quiche I'd bought, and when she didn't answer I looked up and had a bit of a shock. She'd lost all colour in her face and for a moment her stare was completely blank.

"Anna?" I said, "Anna, what's wrong?"

For a moment she didn't answer then said slowly, "Bit of a dizzy turn, that's all, sorry, I'm fine now." By the time I'd got her a glass of water, her colour was indeed returning, and I heaved a sigh of relief, as she had looked dreadful.

She patted my hand. "Not as young as I was, maybe this week's taken more out of me than I thought, sorry, sweetie, if I gave you a fright."

"It's not the usual reaction I get to an invitation." I smiled; she didn't smile back.

"Ellie, this is the silliest coincidence ever, you see I was fostered at Lavender Cottage for a while as a teenager, but it wasn't a good time for me. I was in the care system, labelled a 'troubled child'." She paused, and took a sip of water. "Let's just say I didn't get on well at the cottage, in fact I had to leave and move to another home."

I was puzzled. "How strange, Lottie's spent a lot of time at the cottage, but she's never mentioned your time there."

"Hmm, there are some aspects of my teenage life I'm not that proud of, so I haven't really mentioned them to Lottie – you know how protective us mothers can be?"

I thought briefly that I wasn't sure how well that applied to my own parent, but I reassured Anna, "Honestly, anything you tell me stays just between us. Look, I absolutely understand if you don't fancy coming to the cottage if it's got bad memories for you, please don't worry about it."

She hesitated then said, "Maybe it'd be a good thing for me to see the place restored." She shivered. "In my day it was cold and damp, seeped into your bones, I always felt a chill even when it was warm outside."

"You're not wrong, it was in a dreadful state when I bought it. But kudos to you, Anna, you obviously got over that bad patch and sorted out your life – the wonderful Lottie is living proof."

"Yes of course she is. I suppose one of the really tough things about leaving the cottage was having to leave my whole vinyl collection – I had to start over from scratch again once I was settled in Leeds."

I gasped, reaching over to grab her hand. "I don't believe this! Anna, I found boxes full of old vinyl from the 80s, you must have them back."

"Wow," she said then after a moment's silence, "I don't know what to say, who'd have thought they'd still be there. But not to worry, sweetheart, I duplicated most of them, and I'm just thrilled they've now got a lovely new owner." And she squeezed my hand as it held hers.

"So," I asked, "Are we on for tonight?" Her infectious smile was back.

"We are, because it's probably about time I confronted my demons, what time do you want me?"

I got back to the cottage ahead of Anna who had an errand to run first, which gave me time for a quick tidy up. I'd changed into a simple low cut V-neck t-shirt and skinny black jeans, and saw in the mirror as I ran a comb through my hair that the low neckline left my mole exposed. I wondered if Anna would comment. As I heard her car on the gravel outside and went to welcome her I felt some trepidation, as she'd obviously had a bad experience here, and I didn't want to see her brought low again. I needn't have worried though, she seemed back to her usual exuberant self, greeting me with a kiss and an expensive bottle of wine, coincidentally identical to one I already had chilling in the fridge.

As I showed her round, she was gratifyingly complimentary, exclaiming with delight at the many changes, though when we got to my bedroom it turned out that it had also been hers. She scanned the room closely, and I wondered if she was reliving a time she'd deliberately put to the back of her mind.

She moved slowly across to Hettie's pictures, now framed on the wall. "These are familiar, who's the artist? No, that's a silly question, they look really old. Where did you get them?"

"A local gallery," I said, because the real explanation was too darn complicated.

"18th century, I should think." She was studying them closely, a small frown between her brows.

"Not sure, but yes certainly old." I felt oddly protective of Hettie's artwork. As we headed back downstairs, she was full of praise.

"You've worked wonders, Ellie, I'm so impressed."

"I tried to keep the 18th-century charm, but with 21st-century luxury."

"You've certainly succeeded – love it." She paused. "Funny question, do you ever smell smoke outside?"

I looked at her in surprise. "Yes, I have smelt smoke several times, but haven't found the source, I don't even have any near neighbours."

"I never found out where it was coming from either," she said, then there was a brief pause but when she didn't add anything. I gestured to the couple of boxes of vinyl I'd brought down.

"How about looking through these before we eat? I'm afraid I haven't been very organised, I haven't even decided on the best place for them." She squeezed my arm affectionately, planted herself on the rug and started rifling through as I handed her a glass of the wine I'd chilled, and settled back on the sofa to watch her, delighted at her pleasure.

After a moment or two she looked up. "This is amazing, I can't believe it, these really are all my old records, see, I always made an identifying mark on the corner of the cover, if I lent them to friends, it always meant I could get them back."

"You must have them all back," I said.

"Absolutely not, I know they're in a good home and you'll take good care of them."

"Are you sure?"

"Of course, I told you, all replaced now. Here why don't we put this on?" She handed me Kate Bush, *The Kick Inside*, her debut album, what a coincidence. It was funny how there seemed to be a real thing about Kate Bush around here.

I placed it on the turntable. "Lottie and I love this one too. My favourite track is 'Wuthering Heights'."

"I've always loved her since I saw her sing on *Top of the Pops* when I was a teenager, in fact Lottie was brought up on Kate Bush." I nodded, "she did say." As the music started, Anna grinned in delight as she settled back on the sofa with her wine. "Nothing beats that crackle!" I smiled back, delighted to have a happy guest, and moved into the kitchen to take covers off the food I'd put out.

I'd left my sketches of the Gothic 80s girl from my dream on the coffee table, and next time I glanced over, I saw Anna looking through them studying each one, seemingly lost in thought, then as she shifted on the sofa, putting another cushion behind her back, she noticed my old crocheted blanket flung over the back of the sofa. I'd given it a much-needed wash and forgotten to take it back upstairs. It was the comfort blanket I'd had as a child, weaving my fingers into the crochet holes. It was old even before it got to me and was now sadly threadbare, but it wasn't something I'd ever throw away. Anna had picked up the blanket and buried her face in it; that was weird, was she smelling it? I was thankful it had only just come out of the wash, but even so it wasn't the sort of thing guests usually did. I cleared my throat and she looked up.

"Sorry," she said, "You must think I'm quite mad." I shook my head politely. "It just reminded me of something so similar I had years ago." She did look shaken and I felt ashamed for immediately labelling her a weirdo.

"You look as if you could do with some food inside you," I said. She smiled, nodded and seated herself at the table, but as I leaned forward to hand her a plate, my t-shirt fell away a little and I saw her notice the mole on my breast. She suddenly stood up, so abruptly that I jumped. I mean it was a coincidence, but hardly merited such shock. For a moment we simply stared at each other. The colour had drained from her face, the way it had in the morning, in the shop. She looked as if she might pass out. She began to cry.

I led her back to the sofa, and fetched her some tissues; obviously her returning to the cottage had been one very big mistake, I could have kicked myself. I put my arm round her shaking shoulders, waited until the sobs subsided just a little, then went to get her glass of wine from the table. She took a shaky sip, blew her nose, and said, "Ellie, I think I might be your mother." I sighed. God, this was embarrassing, she'd always seemed so stable, but now I could see memories stirred by the cottage had just knocked all the sense out of her.

"Anna," I said gently, "I think you're upset and confused, my mother is alive and kicking and living in Surrey." I nearly added, 'and as stroppy as ever', but felt levity at this point might be a bit out of place.

"I can see what you're thinking," she said as she began to compose herself. I sincerely hoped she couldn't, but she continued. "You're thinking I'm some kind of a crazy lady, but I have to tell you what happened here, at Lavender Cottage." She turned and picked up the blanket again, held it against her. "This blanket belonged to my foster mother, it was what I wrapped you in when they came to take you away."

I got up from the sofa and went to get my own glass of wine. It wasn't just Anna who needed support. She watched me anxiously as I came back and sat down, waiting for me to speak, and when I didn't, she continued,

"I didn't have a choice, you have to know I had no choice."

"Look," I said, "I understand what you are saying, you were pregnant and had a child, and being here has brought all that back, but that baby wasn't me." She leaned forward and picked up my sketches from the table.

"Ellie, this is me."

"No, it's not, it's just someone I dreamt about. She's not real."

"She is, or rather she was. This is me as a teenager, it's like looking at a photograph, you really have an extraordinary talent, you've caught me exactly."

I shook my head. "No I haven't, it was just a dream I had, and in my dream she was so dreadfully sad, which is the only reason I remembered her, wanted to capture that on paper."

Anna finished her glass of wine and put it down before she spoke again.

"She was sad, she was heartbroken, her baby had been taken away." She reached over, pulling a little at my t-shirt, at the same time pulling her own jumper down fractionally, to where the tiny mark on my breast was identical in shape, size, colour and position to hers. "I noticed your birthmark the moment you were born," she said softly, "And that's not the only thing I've handed down to you, is it?" I stared at her. Of all the strange experiences I'd had over the last couple of years, this was by far and away the most mind-numbing. She took my hand in hers.

"Lottie told me about the hidden chest you found, the cellar, the book. What she didn't know was that I knew they were there. I found them myself when I was living here."

I knew I was still just staring at her, my head was spinning, and I didn't think it was the wine, but it wasn't helping my thinking processes one little bit.

"So wait," I said. "Are you telling me the writing on the bookmarks is yours?" She nodded.

"And when you say 'handed down' does that mean you're a witch?" She nodded again.

"And you're convinced you're my birth mother?"

"Ellie, conviction doesn't come into it, can you not feel the energy?" She raised our joined hands and sure enough, the air around them seemed to have altered subtly; there was brightness there, and a hum, almost too low to hear but when she let me go, there was no doubting the change as the air around us reverted to normal and there was a moment's silence as I allowed all I'd been told to slowly sink in. Then, because I didn't know when I'd next get the chance to ask, "My father? You haven't told me who he was."

She looked down to where her hands now lay folded in her lap, avoiding my gaze.

"There was a group of us who went around together and to be honest, he was more of a friend than a lover. You must remember we were both so young. When I moved away we didn't keep in touch. And no," she put up a hand to forestall my inevitable question, "he knew nothing about my pregnancy, I was so skinny, no one knew, apart from my foster mother."

"Look, I know how painful this all is for you," I said softly, "But I have to know, what was his name?"

"Danny," she said, "Danny Myers. I'm afraid none of our group kept in touch, he was in the care system too and that meant constantly moving around, I'm sorry, sweetheart, I have no idea what became of him."

"D'you think, he's still around?"

She shrugged. "No reason why not, he'd only be the same age as me. May have changed his name though, many did who went through the care system, the shame, you know."

One last burning question. "Was he...?"

"Magical?" she interrupted "We were a small tight-knit group precisely because of what we had in common." I closed my eyes for a moment, recalling my dream. I'd seen him, my father had been one of the youths I'd seen. When I opened my eyes, I could see tears in hers. I reached over and gave her a long hug. I knew how hard dredging up the past had been, and I think we were both equally shaken and stunned.

It wasn't surprising that neither of us could summon up much of an appetite and Anna left far earlier than we'd planned, pleading tiredness. I was pretty sure she wouldn't be in a hurry to come back to Lavender Cottage any time soon.

Of course the minute she'd left, into my head surged all the questions I hadn't asked, although they weren't the sort of questions I could ask in the shop. I'd have to wait until we were alone together again; she'd said she'd take me out for dinner tomorrow evening. I'd just have to be patient, it wasn't as if I didn't have enough to think about, and one thought kept resurfacing – I was magical through and through. I went to bed with my mind churning. I didn't think I had a hope in hell of sleeping, but I must have dropped off almost instantly because I was immediately knee-deep in a dream.

It was set in the present, I was at the cottage which was unaccountably full of people talking, drinking, laughing, spilling out into the garden, spilling drinks on the furniture. But I was watching from the outside, I knew I hadn't been invited, even though this was my home, I knew I wouldn't be welcome. The first person I recognised was Anna as a teenager, dressed exactly as I'd seen her in my dream. To my surprise she was sitting and talking to Hettie in her hessian dress and white pinafore. They were deep in conversation, seemingly oblivious to the noise and movement around them. The cottage looked terrible, like a student den; empty wine and beer bottles were strewn around the room, glasses had been used as ashtrays, and the room stank of smoke. The sofa on which Anna and Hettie were sitting was next to the music system and Anna interrupted their conversation to change the record, and 'Night Porter' by Japan filled my ears.

On a sofa opposite the two women, and also deep in conversation, were my friends Alice, Lizzie and Sarah, but however much I tried to attract their attention, they didn't look up. I looked around for any other familiar faces, but recognised none of the mainly black-clad guests. I made my way upstairs. I was frightened. The menace I sensed increased with each step I climbed, and I knew before I walked into my bedroom there was someone already in there. Tall and thin, black clothing accentuating his height, I couldn't see his face, but the threat was palpable. He seemed completely unaware of my presence. What was it he was so urgently searching for? I followed him as he hurried into the other bedroom. In the corner of that room was a box, and coming from it a soft mewing sound which gained volume to a full blown cry. He moved swiftly, bent over then straightened with a very young baby in his arms. The infant gradually quietened. I could see a lot of dark hair and a glimpse of olive skin, and I didn't need to see more, I knew who she was. A crocheted blanket had fallen to the floor; he swooped on that, swiftly wrapped the baby, and headed down the stairs, out the front door and into the darkness of the night – and I woke abruptly with a splitting headache. I had no idea what the detailed dream meant, and still half-asleep took a couple of paracetamol before slipping swiftly back into a deep thankfully dreamless sleep.

CHAPTER 20

Anna's revelation had turned so much of what I thought I knew on its head, and over the next few days she'd told me more about the circumstances of my birth. At this moment in time, I decided that I wouldn't try to find my father, it wouldn't change my life, especially if he didn't know of my existence. I was just processing the fact that I now had a new mother in Anna, and a half-sister in Lottie, that was enough to digest for now. I genuinely didn't blame Anna for anything, she was really only a child herself and in the care system when she had me, and I understood she had no choice. On the other hand, so much was explained about my relationship with my parents, and I was baffled as to why they hadn't told me about the adoption, if not earlier at least when I reached adulthood. They were the ones I was more angry and disappointed with right now.

Obviously Anna didn't want to spring all this on Lottie until she got back from her holiday, but we agreed she had to know that not only were she and I best friends, we were also half-sisters. We were certain Lottie wouldn't judge Anna, and whilst I couldn't deny I was thrilled to find I had a half-sister, there was a small part of me that was envious of the carefree and happy life Lottie had with my birth mother. That life and relationship had been taken away from me by circumstance. I liked Anna so much, and of course we planned to stay in touch and visit but I suspected it was too late to form a proper mother-daughter connection. Although there was no doubt that I'd inherited her strong magical gene, and some physical similarities.

Anna knew I intended to speak to my parents and had begged me to be kind, saying, "I'm sure they always only wanted the best for you." I shook my head; they might have had their reasons but nevertheless, every time I thought about it I felt a body blow as if someone had kicked me hard in the stomach. When I did confront them, it was every bit as distressing as I'd anticipated. I'd made the trip to see them, this wasn't the sort of conversation that could be had over the phone, but long after it was over, things that were said would come back to me, over and over.

"Of course, we knew about your birth mother's background. We felt a clean slate was the best thing for you," my mother said.

I hadn't reacted well. "What the fuck, I deserved to know about my own birth! I've always felt like the cuckoo in the nest. Now I know why – my whole life's just been one big fat lie." I'd taken my blanket with me and it was at that point I threw it at her, and it landed short and lay on the floor between us, a symbol of everything that hurt. A tatty brightly coloured blanket I'd been led to believe was from her own childhood, the thing she'd kept to remind her of what she had achieved after the life she'd left. I felt that was a lie too far, and I said so.

Things went steeply downhill from there. My mother chose to harshly criticise everything from my lack of gratitude to selfishness, and my appalling rudeness, and then went on to cover my fashion sense, where I was living, and the way I was wasting my life. It was a dreadful meeting. As I left, I swore never to go back, and my mother flung the blanket after me and slammed the front door.

Lottie had taken the news well, but there was no doubt our relationship had changed us both in fact and feeling. I knew she'd always had Anna to herself, and I wondered if she might be worried that she'd now have to share her affection with me. It wasn't anything she said, just a sense of things being off between us. Maybe over time it would get better. I didn't want to keep secrets from her, but maybe this was one that would have been better kept just between myself and Anna.

What had happened in my life, had not left me unscathed on the emotional front. I'd gone into a kind of free-fall, I felt like a boat that had mislaid its oars, reduced to drifting aimlessly on the water. I loved my new life, but the unsettled feeling which had been with me as far back as I could remember, had returned. That sense of not quite belonging. But as things went round and round in my head I had to keep telling myself, I no longer had to please anyone but me.

***

I started my university course in October, a welcome distraction. A fresh start I was looking forward to – a chance to stop dwelling on the past and I knew I'd enjoy kick-starting my brain again. I'd had a good student experience the first time around, meeting Alice, Lizzie and Sarah, all of whom had been really supportive when I told them my adoption shock news. They weren't as surprised as they could have been though, they'd all seen first-hand the emotional disconnect between me and my parents, so different from their own families. Alice even commented that at times she'd felt they preferred her to me, hurtful but true.

I drove to the university with my bag packed full of brand new items I'd bought according to the list I'd been sent, parked and headed into the building. I knew I'd be one of the older students by a long shot, but that didn't bother me. I'd been to the induction day, so had familiarised myself with the campus layout, and was pleased to see there was a café already open. Fortified by a banana, a breakfast bar, and a steaming hot latte, I made my way to what was to be my first lecture, relishing the familiarity of the university sounds and smells which were the same the world over.

I opted for a seat at the back of the room, as we all filed in for our first lecture given by Professor Williams. Whilst we waited there was a buzz of conversation, newbies nervously getting to know each other. The girl to my left was Grace, straight from college, while Josh on my right was a little older, he'd had a gap year. The buzz ceased as the professor strode in; he'd not been at the original induction and I was looking forward to his lecture the most, as his area of the syllabus I found most interesting, it covered North Yorkshire myths and legends.

As he swung on his heel and faced us, I felt a tingle of shock, almost recognition, run right through me. He couldn't be further from what I'd expected, from his well-worn-in black Doc Martens to his black battered leather jacket which he took off to reveal a tight-fitting black t-shirt. He took his time, aware all eyes were on him; he knew the impact he had, and the confidence to carry it off. Another, almost painful shock ran through me as he looked up, and silently surveyed us row by row. The startling translucency of his pale skin only emphasised ice blue, wolf-like eyes which gave him an almost otherworldly appearance. I wondered briefly whether they could be contact lenses – now that would be vanity taken to extremes. His hair compounded his unique appearance because although he only looked mid-forties, it was a bright silver grey with only a few darker strands of what I assumed to be the original colour. As his chill glance ran from front to back of the room, there was a collective inhalation of breath. His timing was impeccable. Grace nudged me and made a 'wow' face, as he began to speak.

"Good morning, everyone. I'm Professor Seb Williams, thank you for attending my lecture, and please feel free to call me Seb, I'm not precious about Professor." He paused, and no-one stirred; he had a slight accent I couldn't identify. "So, myths and legends of North Yorkshire. We have a lot to work through. Thoughts or questions we don't get to during our time together, just reach out to me online." I wasn't really taking in what he was saying although he had my complete attention. I was baffled and charmed in equal measure. I'd never even spoken to this deliberately dishevelled man with the just-got-out-of-bed look, and he was certainly not my usual type, but I knew beyond a shadow of a doubt this was seismic, and life after Prof. Seb Williams was never going to be quite the same as it had been before.

As the weeks passed I was able to dismiss any worries I had about keeping up with my younger fellow students. The only module in which I wasn't moving forward as fast as I'd like was Myths and Legends, taken by Seb. No matter what resolutions I made about focusing, concentrating and retaining, his lectures seemed to fly out the window from the moment he started until the moment he walked out the door. Reading my notes afterwards, more often than not what I'd written made no sense at all, in fact often all that was on my page were endless sketches of this fascinating human being. I know it sounds weird. I was everlastingly grateful to Grace, who knocked spots off everyone when it came to note-taking and summarising. I thanked my lucky stars we'd become friends because she was generous and never minded sharing her notes to bring me up to speed. I knew it was because she thought I was having trouble keeping up, and shamelessly traded on that. Don't judge me.

Seb's unusual looks had gained him the nickname Wolf, and this was how everyone referred to him behind his back, although I'm pretty certain he knew and didn't disapprove. Much as I'd have liked him to, he paid me no more attention than any other student, less in fact, I was invisible to him. Maybe he'd decided as an obviously mature student I didn't need nursing along like the others fresh out of college. On the other hand, maybe despite my best efforts, my feelings were showing more than I'd have liked, and he was simply steering clear of the trouble that so often besets tutor-student relationships. I honestly couldn't believe I had a crush on my professor, what a cliché. In my thirties it was the very last thing I'd expected, and I was not thrilled.

I'd been pleasantly surprised at how easily I'd fallen into easy friendships with the other students. I'd been apprehensive they'd look on me as out of touch, being much older, but I couldn't have been more wrong. I think my Goth image helped keep me cool and interesting, a mysterious side to me. They were happy for me to join them on nights out, and over the weeks of that first term, several of them came to me for advice, which I was happy to dish out on all sorts of things that were worrying them, mainly relationship issues; if only they knew!

Nights out were always on a budget, fulfilling the aims of most students to drink as much as possible for the least amount of money. Moving through the town we were always on the alert for Happy Hours or Buy One Get One Free offers. It was a world away from my London days where money or lack of it was never a problem, and on occasion I put some money behind the bar to treat everyone. We all agreed that Wolf's lectures were head and shoulders above some of the others we sat through. The truth or falsehoods of some of the more outlandish tales were debated endlessly, and I often wondered exactly how my classmates would react if they knew the truth about me.

Approaching the end of term, we were all in a demob-happy mood, and took ourselves on a pub crawl around Whitby. Seb was the only tutor who joined us, and this was actually the first time I'd spoken to him apart from brief lecture interactions. He made a beeline for me, although I told myself it was only because the rest of the students were so much younger.

"So, Ellie, I hear you moved from London, what prompted that?"

Heroically rising above the effect he was having on me, desperately hoping he couldn't see the blush rising on my cheeks, I did my best to reply coherently.

"I was in advertising, worked hard, reaped the rewards and thought I was fine. Then I came to Whitby and fell for it like a ton of bricks."

"And uni?" he said.

I laughed. "Never in my wildest dreams did I think I'd go back, I guess I've just become so wrapped up in the history of the area. But how about you? Have you always lived around here?"

"God, no. Spent most of my life in Ireland." Ah, that explained the accent although it was only slight. "Always been fascinated by the myths and legends handed down, some written, most passed orally from one generation to another. I came here because I knew it was a place abounding in legend – and I was hooked." He laughed briefly. "I even did another PhD on the subject, because I knew that would be the sure-fire way of getting it put on the syllabus here. Can I get you another drink?"

I'd drained my glass of wine, and was starting to feel a little woozy, didn't think I wanted to show myself up.

"Could I have something non-alcoholic? This has gone straight to my head, and I didn't have time for lunch today."

"Soda and lime? That's what I'm sticking to."

"Sounds perfect, thank you." I reached for my wallet but he waved it away, and I watched as he made his way towards the bar.

When he handed me the drink, our fingers touched briefly. I felt the chemistry between us, and as we continued to talk, the crowd around us with all their noise and laughter seemed to fade away. Our focus on the conversation and each other lasted until last orders were called, surprising both of us. I retrieved my phone from my bag, and he raised an eyebrow.

"Just calling a cab," I said, "I didn't bring the car tonight."

"Well if you tell me the whereabouts of this wonderful cottage you've been talking about, I'll give you a lift." Maybe I was more drunk than I thought. I hadn't told him about the cottage, had I?

"Err... It's in Eastcombe, but really, I don't want to take you out of your way."

"You're not, I don't live too far from there." For some reason I didn't believe his response, but I ignored my head, and listened to my heart.

"Thank you, that's very kind," I said as we made our way out of the pub, and I studiously ignored a couple of groups of my student friends, and hoped to God Seb didn't see Grace give me a wink and a thumbs up sign. As we walked across the dark car park, I stumbled over a dip in the ground and Seb took my elbow. The musky aroma of his aftershave sent yet another tingle down my spine.

As he drove, we made small talk until I started to direct him once we got near the cottage. When we pulled into the drive he frowned for a brief second, then turned to me accusingly.

"You never said it was Lavender Cottage!"

"You didn't ask."

"Good God, girl, do you know all the stories about this place?"

"Not when I bought it." I admitted. "But I've found out a hell of a lot since."

"And now you're spooked?"

I laughed. "Don't you believe it, I'm just fascinated, and it all adds to the charm."

"Bet you got it at a good price." He commented, "Superstitious lot around here wouldn't have touched it with a bargepole."

"I did," I said, hesitated then added, "If you'd like to have a look round?"

"I'll pass tonight, Ellie, but maybe another time?" he said and I couldn't decide whether I was glad or disappointed. I certainly felt a little snubbed because up till now all our conversation had been so easy, but it was clearly back to tutor-student status as he said, "'Night, Ellie." And drove off.

After that evening, in lectures, when our glances crossed, he turned away quickly, desperate not to lock eyes with me even for a few seconds. But I knew he was interested, and for whatever reason he wouldn't admit it to himself, or was I that deluded? I also knew I'd fallen heavily for him, and as long as I avoided repeating Alice's mistake, an unwanted pregnancy, I saw no reason for not moving forward. There was no denying the deep connection I felt, which echoed that small shock of recognition the first time I'd seen him. Without wanting to sound too Mills and Boon, it felt to me as if he could see into my soul. Out of the corner of my eye I'd seen him staring at me when he thought I wasn't looking.

By the time we reached the last day of term, I was only too ready to stop. I was looking forward to relaxing over the Christmas holidays, two weeks of chilling at the cottage, and I'd deliberately made hardly any social arrangements other than meeting some of the single Mystical Ladies for Christmas dinner. Beth had arranged to meet at the Quirky Den, the tiniest pub in town, for pre-dinner drinks; they were opening for a choice few on Christmas Day. It was situated on Grape or Grope Lane as we all called it. We would then head for The Star Inn by the harbour for dinner. I was looking forward to it. Seb must have been feeling a bit of the Christmas spirit today because he let us go early. Daydreaming, I wondered how he was spending the Christmas break; would he be on his own? The rest of the group who I couldn't help thinking of as the youngsters, were out of there at breakneck speed, desperate to hit the pub. I wasn't up for joining them, but as I packed my books away I planned to hit the shops on the way home to stock up and make sure I wasn't caught short if we were hit hard with snow.

When Seb spoke, I jumped. I thought he'd left with everyone else but if he had, he'd now come back.

"Ellie, I'd really like to come and see Lavender Cottage, if that's OK with you?" I wasn't sure whether he meant he wanted to see me, or was in fact just interested in a bit of historical architecture.

"No problem at all, whenever it suits you," I said.

"Would it be too soon if I came today? As long as you haven't got any other plans?"

I instantly dropped all thought of stocking up for Christmas, and nodded. "No, no plans, I was just going to get home and chill all evening." I could have bitten my tongue; had I given him too big a hint that he could stay longer? I felt butterflies in my stomach, that was definitely not my style.

"Great, I just need to finish up a few things, I'll see you there shortly."

The first thing that hit me as I got home was thank goodness Cynthia had been today, whatever she'd used smelt lush. The cushions were nicely plumped, and white lilies in the pewter vase on the dining table added their own fragrance. Bless her heart, she'd hiked up the heating so the cottage felt wonderfully warm after the winter chill outside. I put a match to the kindling in the fireplace. I didn't need the warmth, but loved the feeling of cosiness it imparted. I also lit a couple of candles, then worried that it all looked too contrived. *Pull yourself together*, I said to myself, *he's interested in the cottage for historic relevance, that's all.* But when I opened the door to him, I noticed that he had made an effort of sorts, changing his t-shirt, doing something with that hair, and the musky aftershave hit me again.

"Come on in," I said and wondered if the smile he flashed could be classed as wicked. As he took in the open plan room, it felt like he was breathing in the atmosphere, and for a few moments there was an awkward silence.

He spoke first. "What you've achieved is outstanding, you must be so proud of yourself. It genuinely feels like I've stepped back in the 18th century, yet," he waved a hand, "We're surrounded by all mod cons."

"I'll give you the tour if you like, but it won't take long." I had a few seconds' doubt as I said it, but reasoned I was only leading him upstairs for historic interest. He was indeed keen to explore each room, murmuring with delight at all the original features I'd managed to preserve. Running his hand along some of the panelling, he turned to me jokingly.

"Find any secret hidey holes? You know how much smuggling and goodness only knows what else went on round here?"

I lied, smiling. I'd become extremely accomplished at concealing those facts I wanted to conceal. "Sadly no, the builder had a good look too, and we opened up the cellar but all we got was cold and damp." I deliberately changed the subject as we descended the stairs. "Can I get you a cup of coffee?"

"Proper, or instant?" he said with a mock frown, "I warn you I'm a coffee snob."

I blessed the deli. "Relax, I have a very good machine and some very good coffee," and as I moved into the kitchen area I called back over my shoulder, "How do you like it?"

"Strong as you like, with sugar, no milk." He hadn't taken a seat but was prowling the room, appreciating every little nook and cranny. It would appear that his interest was definitely the cottage and not its owner.

Unbidden, a wicked idea hit me, I'd been given a rather special something from a friend in town; most customers to her shop walked away with herbal lotions and potions, but for Sisters there was always something special. She'd grinned when she gave it to me.

"In case you need it one of these days. Just a drop will do the trick." Surely, I reasoned, it couldn't do any harm to try, it might not be the most ethical way of attracting someone, but what if that person just needed a shove in the right direction? I'd never used any of these myself and knew they didn't always work, but Lottie had confessed she'd used one on Luke. She'd explained that because the potion only worked where there was attraction in the first place, and she could see no harm in it, she already knew she and Luke were going to be together, this just gave an extra small push. Despite that, once I'd carefully added the drop and we were seated on two sofas opposite each other, I felt uneasy.

He'd nodded approvingly with the first sip. "Nice." He helped himself to one of the biscuits I'd put out, and leaned back again. "You know, Ellie, it's bizarre, and you'll think I'm mad, but it feels as if I've been here before, it's all so familiar. You ever get a feeling like that?"

I could hardly say to him 'that might be because you're my soulmate', so instead said lightly, "Of course, déjà vu, I think everyone has it now and then, but I do know what you mean in relation to this cottage, I felt it the first time I saw it. In fact, still feel that way."

I could see he was making a conscious effort to keep things on a mundane level. Was he a true gentleman or just playing a game? I had no idea and as he carried on quietly drinking his coffee, wanted to break the silence but couldn't think how. I finished my coffee and on impulse went back to the kitchen and helped myself to a glass of wine. I indicated the bottle to him but he shook his head, and I went to put on a record. It seemed to be what was needed because it led to a discussion of music and bands we liked, as well as those we didn't, and of course that led on to the vinyl collection I'd found.

"How strange," he said, "That somebody just left it, wonder who the owner was."

I shook my head. "No idea." I didn't feel it was sensible to share what I'd learned from Anna, so turned the conversation towards my current obsession with 80s music.

When he put his cup back on the table, looked at his watch and made to rise, I wasn't surprised, I could see how unrelaxed he was.

"I think you've chosen well here," he said, "You and the cottage suit each other. Thank you for the tour, but I've kept you long enough." I made a polite protestation as he continued, "Enjoy the holidays, and see you in the new term." Standing at the open door, so the light could illuminate the way to his car, I reflected on the utter uselessness of the potion I'd given him. Time to give up, and accept he was my history professor, nothing more. It was clear that if he was interested, it was in the cottage not me.

CHAPTER 21

January

Returning to lectures after the Christmas break was in the bleakest of weathers. Snow had come in across the moors making it difficult to get out of the village, and because many of the other students were in a similar situation, most of the lectures had been cancelled and notes sent so we could work from home.

My New Year's resolution had been to forget my obsession with Seb, although that was easier said than done. But I knew I was wasting my time and energy. Maybe he was already in a relationship, married, not interested in mixing business with pleasure or just plain not interested. There was also the fact that I was one of his students. Luckily, I liked my own company and had to admit I really didn't need any complications in my life. My social life could be as busy or as relaxed as I wanted, and I made up my mind to simply put my head down and concentrate on my studies.

I was getting good marks and working hard, making an effort to avoid staring at Seb during lectures. There was no doubt in my mind that we had a deep connection, despite his unwillingness to acknowledge it. I tried to think of him as no different to all the other tutors. Unfortunately, dreams can't be controlled in the same way, and let's just say I was having some that were pretty risqué!

My friendship with Lottie had gone back to being comfortable again and we'd had some real heart-to-heart conversations, along with quite a few tears as we both adjusted to our new relationship.

The Mystical Ladies were still meeting regularly at Lavender Cottage, and I loved having them over. At our first meeting of the year, the discussion turned to love potions, and in view of the failure of the one I'd used, I listened closely. Victoria, one of the younger, quieter witches didn't come to every meeting and when she did, tended to keep herself to herself. I hadn't really got to know her. At that January meeting she was there and raised the subject.

"Do you all think love potions are ethical – I mean you're technically getting someone to do something against their will, aren't you?"

Hazel, who never hesitated to speak her mind, tutted. "Victoria, we've used them from generation to generation with no real harm. Honestly, I sometimes think the world's gone completely mad, unethical, my foot!" Then I heard her mumble under her breath, "Snowflakes".

But Victoria obviously had concerns, and was quite prepared to stand up to Hazel, "Isn't it like having your drink spiked in a bar?" It was clear Hazel was becoming more heated by the minute and was squaring up for a confrontation. Witches hate to be questioned on spells, and many of them viewed the new generation as being ridiculously politically correct.

Luckily Lottie waded in to avert a row. "I'm not ashamed to admit I used a love potion on Luke, only a low grade, no harm done, love grew from there and look where we are now." There was a mutter of muted comment around the room, and I seized the moment to ask, "What if a potion just doesn't work, asking for a friend of course?"

"Ellie," laughed Beth, "I thought you were happily single."

"Oh, it was a while back, and nothing came of it, that's why I asked."

Lottie gave me a sideways glance. "Doesn't always work immediately, Ellie, give it time."

Late March

On the last day of the spring term we were all meeting up in town, although to be truthful the novelty of going out with the younger students had rather worn off. I decided I'd join them for just a couple of drinks and then meet up with Lottie, staying over at hers to save getting a cab back. Making my way to the bar, I noticed Seb was already there, surrounded by a group of students. He hadn't seen me, and I watched as they vied for his attention. It had crossed my mind on more than one occasion that he might be a bit of a player; after all there were plenty of gorgeous girls on the course.

Taking my drink, I joined another group of students until they decided it was time to move on, then I made my excuses. I was meeting Lottie in under half an hour, so I grabbed one of the outside tables and although I rarely smoked these days, lit a cigarette and sat back to enjoy the lovely spring evening. Scrolling through my phone, I realised someone was approaching. Seb; my heart skipped a beat.

"Can I get you a drink?" He indicated my currently empty glass.

"A glass of Sauvignon would be nice. Thank you."

I was aware of a warm glow and I didn't think it was due to my previous couple of glasses. He certainly seemed far more relaxed than the last time we were on our own together. When he returned with the drinks, I offered him a cigarette, ignoring the effect caused by the brush of his hand against mine, and we chatted about nothing in particular – the weather, uni news, plans for the upcoming break, until he said, "You know, you offered to show me around your garden and that fascinating forest on your doorstep, any chance you're free on Saturday?" Again, I didn't remember offering to show him round anywhere but wasn't prepared to look a gift horse in the mouth.

"You mean tomorrow, right?"

"If you're free?"

"I am," I said, then added, "Perhaps you'd like to stay for supper?"

"Great. How about if I get to you around 4.00, it should still be light."

"Sounds good." We sat quietly for a few minutes in a comfortable silence until he got up to go.

"OK, see you tomorrow."

By the time Seb arrived the following day, I still hadn't quite made up my mind whether or not I should be honest with him about my feelings. One half of me said yes, the other said, don't risk it. I was still dithering as we moved into the garden. He seemed genuinely interested and was brushing his hand over the herbs as we strolled, rubbing his fingers together on leaves of mint, lavender, and thyme.

"Lovely," he said, inhaling the various scents. "Were you behind the planning?"

"Not really, I just knew what I wanted – lots of herbs and the sort of flowers that would recreate an 18th-century cottage garden. The real expert was my gardener, I told him what I had in mind and he did the rest."

The sun was slowly setting as we made our way to the edge of my land. I'd forgotten how much it had rained recently and whilst I had my Hunter wellies on, Seb just had normal footwear, which were soon mud-coated although he didn't seem to mind. As we walked there was a fresh aroma of damp moss and pine from the trees on the border of my land, and with the sun moving even lower, dusk was setting in. Reaching the river we stood silently side by side as, swollen by recent rain, it flowed fast at our feet. Memories of my dreams and Hettie's demise came to mind, and for a moment I felt fearful. There was a distinct chill in the air, and I shivered involuntarily, thankful I wasn't alone. Seb was standing unnaturally still, rooted to the spot and I wondered what he was thinking.

He seemed to give himself a mental shake, turning to me. "How amazing you have all this." He looked down at the fast-flowing current. "I've always been fascinated by water, could spend the whole day just watching." I nodded; this was all well and good, but I was getting colder by the minute, although I felt it would be impolite just to turn and start walking back. He didn't seem inclined to move. "I've always loved the musicality of flowing water," he murmured, "Magical, isn't it?" He then said, "We could cross the river over there, and walk further into the forest?" I said with another shiver going down my spine, "Perhaps we should start heading back now, it's getting dark, and I'd feel really silly if we got lost in the forest." He laughed; was I imagining it, or did he have a strange look in his eyes? "We wouldn't want that," he said.

At the front door he removed his muddy shoes and in answer to my concerned look smiled, "Don't worry, I have a spare pair in the boot." I discarded my own wellies, leaving them next to his shoes, and hurried into the warmth. Seb was making himself comfortable on one of the leather sofas. I offered him a drink, but as he was driving he opted for a sensible coffee. Glancing over my shoulder, I could see he was soaking up the atmosphere. He seemed just as fascinated by my home as the first time he'd visited, but this time I'd made up my mind, no magic added. I'd been disconcerted by Victoria's concerns about love spells being unethical, and it hadn't worked anyway. As I handed him the cup and saucer, I noticed with inner amusement he was wearing odd socks; that was definitely a professor sort of thing.

When I put a dark chill-out playlist on Spotify, one of my favourites came on. As 'Bathroom Girl', by Air played, I wondered if I should have gone for something more cheerful but he said, "I love this track, the gloomier the music, the better my mood."

"Same here!" I said, "Must be something in the water round here, anything that pulls on the heart strings seems to suit the mood of the cottage." Looking up from my latte, I realised he was staring at me. Having convinced myself he was only here to look at the garden, I had to readjust to the fact that something might have changed. As the music became darker, the atmosphere became more charged, then without a word he carefully put his coffee cup down on the table and moved across to sit alongside me on the sofa. Gently taking my cup away, not taking his eyes off me, he put his hands either side of my face and moved in for a lingering delicious kiss. For a split second, I wondered if the love potion had actually worked after all – Lottie had said give it time – or if this had been inevitable. As I followed him silently up to my room, I knew I'd finally lured him into the spider's web, magic or no magic.

Making love with Seb was like nothing I'd experienced before, I knew we had a connection, I just didn't expect it to be this mind-blowing, and I knew it was mutual. This was our destiny as I'd seen it all along. We were soul mates. Lying in my bed, the bedcovers messy around us, I saw a brief look of satisfaction on his face before it changed to one of remorse, even regret? "Seb?"

"I'm sorry, this wasn't meant to happen! I honestly came round to see the garden, that's the truth."

"Of course you did," I agreed, grinning.

"It's the truth, Ellie, this was a big mistake! I've tried so hard to resist you, but you're intoxicating. I shouldn't have come over today."

"Well," I said, "No regrets from me, what just happened was amazing, it was meant to be, can't you see that?"

He gently brushed the hair from my eyes. "I'm sorry, Ellie, I just can't get involved. The timing isn't right, it's complicated, I can't explain."

"Shit, you're married?" My heart sank; this wasn't how I'd seen it panning out, but I was pretty certain, married or not, he wouldn't be able to resist next time, and although I had a rule about not messing with married guys, I was prepared to break it for Seb.

He sighed and shook his head. "No I'm not married, but..." he paused and shook his head again, "There's something about you, you've drawn me in, it's like I already know you so well."

"I feel it too," I said softly, "I think we've met before – not sure if you believe in that sort of thing, but I do."

He shrugged, "I don't know, I can't explain it."

We moved back downstairs, both of us exhausted, and I put together a mezze platter. He watched me as he ate; he needed to get some energy back, but even just watching him eat was highly charged. I wanted to ask him more; maybe there was someone else in his life and he didn't want to say, or he was just letting me down gently, this was just a one-night stand. Finishing the meal, he wiped his mouth and was first to break the silence, almost as if he was reading my mind.

"This can't be repeated," he said, "However much I might want it to." I stayed silent, I knew he'd be back but he definitely felt uncomfortable now. "I'm afraid I have to go, thank you for supper." His complicated situation, whatever it was, wouldn't stop us. I knew it and so did he.

CHAPTER 22

6 Months Later

Our passionate, frenzied, all-consuming relationship continued, very much behind closed doors. More precisely behind the closed doors of Lavender Cottage. I hadn't been invited over to his place, and had started to feel a little like Seb's dirty little secret. Does that bear out the 'Be careful what you wish for' warning? He had insisted on the secrecy, which I understood to some extent, our teacher-student relationship, but it seemed more than that somehow, I couldn't put my finger on it. I'd reached a stage where there were niggling voices at the back of my head, and as time went on, they got louder. I argued against them. I was with the guy of my dreams, what could be so wrong about that? Unless of course he was the man of my nightmares? One part of me insisted there was something wrong and I should get out, the other part of me was determined not to listen. Talk about conflicted, I couldn't give him up, even if I wanted to.

I'd taken Seb at his word and told nobody about our affair, so couldn't share my dilemma, and it was easy to hide behind the phone with the girls, keeping my posts light – stories about uni, the other students, that sort of thing. Lottie on the other hand was a different kettle of fish altogether, she knew something wasn't right. I invented all sorts of reasons not to see her, and was aware I was gradually withdrawing from all those who'd come to mean a lot to me. I wasn't myself, but couldn't seem to stop, I was addicted.

There was one break in my increasingly clandestine life. About five months into our relationship, he took me out one night to an old tavern owned by a friend of his, some miles outside of our locality. Apparently this guy was discreet, so Seb deemed it safe, they went back a long way. The inn ironically was called The Witches Brew, and we had a great evening, which made me all the more frustrated we didn't do it more often; it was so good to get out. The inn itself was over 400 years old, with an actual witching post built into the beams. I was fascinated by the stories his friend had to tell about his clientele; dark and mystical stories. The inn had been blessed by a priest to ward off witches when it was first built, although fast forward to today and there was a witch's broomstick on the wall. The landlord Jim explained solemnly it had belonged to his mother who always wore black, and died on Halloween. Prior to departing this earth she'd insisted on parking her broomstick in the pub, so he wouldn't forget her. Of course we all laughed heartily, sure it was a joke, although I sensed an odd undertone, or maybe that was just my conscience pricking me about the secrets I was keeping.

Sadly the evening out wasn't repeated, and there could be no doubt I was seeing more of the dark and brooding Seb and less of the lighter, teasing mood I loved. He professed undying love, at the same time encouraging my increasing isolation. 'I want to keep you to myself,' he'd say, and it was true, we were cocooned in our own world. I suppose the danger signs were there though from the start, if I'd cared to see them. As time went on 'Be careful what you wish for,' popped into my mind ever more frequently. But I'd got what I wanted, and allowed myself to be pulled willingly into what was, I came to recognise too late, dangerously unacceptable behaviour. I also realised he knew so much about my life, he knew about the group of 'friends' who came over once a month for drinks, my relationship with Lottie, my nights out with Will and friends, but I knew nothing about Seb outside of his work at uni.

One evening we were sitting having drinks listening to Serge Gainsborough and Jane Birkin's 'Je t'aime'. The mood was certainly romantic, and I felt totally relaxed until he spoke.

"Ellie," he started, and I guessed this was going to be something other than sweet nothings. "I think you should stop having your friends over every month." I didn't know what to say, but he knew I wouldn't argue with him. "You're my delicious secret, you know I love you, and we can't risk anyone finding out about us." I wanted to ask why, but instead I sat silently as he continued. "And,

Will, I'm concerned you're seeing too much of him and his friends." Seb knew Will because they'd done a history project together. Pulling me closer he said, "I think you need to cut down, he's very perceptive, we can't risk him drawing any conclusions." I didn't say anything and he added, "You do know I'm only saying this for your own good, right?" I nodded; he was being extremely possessive, but he loved me, wanted me to himself. Nothing wrong with that.

Deep down and unacknowledged was the understanding I was being too compliant, but our passion was so intense, who wouldn't want to be loved that much? How we managed to appear normal during lectures, I don't know, and it wasn't easy. By this time, the only people I was seeing were my uni friends. Seb felt that was safe, after all, they were only interested in getting wasted as cheaply as possible on nights out, nothing else, besides which Seb usually came with us now. He'd keep a low profile, talking to everyone other than me. But I was always aware, with a delicious shiver, of those wolf eyes on me all evening, especially when I spoke to other guys.

Seb seemed as obsessed by my home as he was with me. I often jokingly teased I wasn't sure who he loved most, me or the cottage. He'd been doing his own research, building up a complete picture of its history. His intense interest, I have to confess, made me feel a little suffocated, and as time moved on I was convinced he was snooping when I wasn't in the room. And there were still frequent questions about hiding places.

"I can't believe you didn't find any, what with its incredible history."

"I told you before," I said, "Ted would have found it, he ripped the place apart, even the cellar." Seb smiled in a way that, had I been less besotted, I might have seen as smug. "You'd be surprised at some of the ingenious hiding places, we need to persevere." And persevere he did, sighing with frustration, as he felt his way around the stone walls downstairs for the umpteenth time.

I was definitely starting to feel hemmed in as well as loved up. I started to feel trapped, I'd never had this intense a relationship before. None of my previous relationships had lasted much longer than six months, but I didn't want it to finish, I was drowning in desire, and turmoil at the same time. I knew for certain we were soul mates, but I was changing as a person, no longer feeling carefree, I was half the woman I'd been, anxious to please all the time. But then I reasoned when he was critical it was for my own good.

Even so I was taken aback when one night he arrived quite late, by cab and pretty much the worse for wear, and said he would be moving in! He had a course to attend first, so wouldn't be able to bring everything over for a few days, and I was shocked. He hadn't even asked, just made the assumption I wanted him to live at the cottage. I felt both exhilaration and dread. Wasn't it what I wanted, though? Seb all to myself? We were destined to be together, soul mates, although at the back of my mind there was a small voice murmuring that even soul mates like to be consulted.

His attitude changed from that point. He became even more silent and morose. He didn't share his feelings with me, and the more I tried to recapture what we had, the more he pushed me away, but I couldn't live without him. I'd never felt this way about anyone, maybe part of the attraction was the insecurity, I craved his approval. Small things though added to my unease, I couldn't quite pin down what though, as he'd never laid a finger on me, never touched me in a violent way, or even raised his voice. But then he didn't need to, he had psychological control. I'd always thought I was super strong, but he seemed to unerringly find my weak spots. I knew I was complicit in his coercive behaviour, and of course because we'd kept our relationship secret, there was no-one I could talk to, confide in, and an unsettling thought wormed into my head; had I caused all this with my love potion? Would it have just been a harmless infatuation if I'd left well alone, not meddled?

Seb was essentially a loner, a true academic, his head in an historical cloud most of the time. He'd often wander beyond the cottage garden to the river and forest beyond, finding his own space. I'd potter in the garden, cutting flowers and herbs to fragrance the house, or make something for us to eat, between my own studies. Apart from attending lectures I was spending more and more time in the cottage, virtually becoming a hermit myself. I didn't ever again accompany Seb to the river, I wasn't happy around the water, dreams of drowning always in the back of my mind. Seb, however, always came back from the water as if he'd been energised.

I had made up my mind that the time had probably come, indeed passed, to tell my friends about him, but was honestly unsure how to describe him and our relationship. Moody, non-communicative, intense and deeply intelligent, a bit of a brooding Heathcliff character. Stating facts such as 'doesn't suffer fools gladly,' or 'doesn't really have the charm gene,' didn't sound particularly enhancing either.

CHAPTER 43

Even once he'd made the decision to move in, Seb didn't want to be seen out in public with me. We'd never been out for another date night despite all the great restaurants in town. Maybe I'd suggest it when he was settled in? I was certainly becoming more frustrated at being hidden away.

The evening before he left for the London conference, we had a wonderful evening; he was an awesome lover, and I'd made an extra special effort, a new sheer silk dress, musky smelling candles in the bedroom, fairy lights twinkling around the bed. It did occur to me that once he moved in and undertook everyday tasks, we might lose a little of the romance. Leaving Seb in the shower, I came downstairs to sort out supper. Feeling tired but sated, I was ravenous and thirsty too. As I took a long drink of water, I noticed his phone on the coffee table. He never normally left it lying around, but now it flashed a message.

It wasn't in my nature to spy, I wasn't suspicious or jealous; I was nosy though and a step or two let me see what was on the screen. The message was oddly titled – The Purge, and it was from Will. Was that my Will? I wasn't able to open the message but could read part of the message on the screen.

How's it going with E, you getting there?

My heart seemed to stop for a moment then pounded, as I heard Seb coming out of the shower upstairs and I instantly put the phone back on the table. Who was E? Was that me? Surely not. And The Purge, maybe it was some research he was doing. I couldn't breathe properly, my head was spinning, my scalp icy cold and then everything went blacker than black.

I opened my eyes to find I was in the garden of the cottage, but not, I knew beyond a doubt, in my own time. That door to the past had opened again, I was back in Hettie's time. The scene was so familiar, reds, yellows and magenta leaves on the trees, the very faint sound of the river running beyond, and the unmistakable chill and scent of autumn in the air. I swung round to the cottage, and walked the cobbled path to the front door. As I moved quietly from room to room, I could feel how empty it seemed. Personal possessions were no longer cluttered around, and there were few pieces of furniture, it looked as if everything had been hurriedly stripped away, leaving nothing of the warmth, and delicious cooking smells I remembered from before. But then I realised there were glowing embers in the fireplace, and a lit candle in the corner of the room. I heard a sound coming from upstairs, and this visit seemed different somehow, the whole experience more intense. I ran upstairs into what was now my bedroom; the dragging sound had stopped, but in a corner of the bedroom Hettie was sitting on a stool, sobbing, head in hands. By her side was the wooden trunk, the one I'd found in the secret room, and she was packing it with all her worldly goods.

As she became aware of my presence she jumped up, her pale face, whitening even more.

"Ellie! You can't be here. You have to leave, it's not safe. He's coming for me." She moved across the room, her hand on my arm shaking.

"Who, Hettie?"

"Abe." She whispered the name as if uttering it might summon him sooner.

"Who..." I started, but she laid a swift finger over my lips.

"Go, Ellie, just go." There was fear in her voice, and I shivered. Whoever this man was, he obviously terrified her.

She moved away. "I have to finish packing, my cousin will come with his cart to pick up the trunk, I'm going to join my mother and daughter." She looked around, saying, "I think I have everything, although in truth I know I am not thinking clearly."

"Tell me..." I started but she interrupted, "Ellie, the hate. The hate is rising again, they are purging the witches, I have eyes and ears in the village, it is he who is behind the hate. And..." she faltered for a moment, "And people who've known me for years, now believe what he tells them." A memory stirred; purging, I'd heard that word recently.

"He promised me the world, told me he loved me. After I had his child, he was going to leave his wife, but it never happened, and now," she gave a dry sob, "Now he is at the forefront of the witch hunts."

"Hettie, they can't take the law into their own hands, there must be somebody you can go to?"

She laughed, a humourless sound. "The village has its own laws, always has done, always will. What happens here for good or ill stays." She lowered her voice, again. "The threat is real, there are others, women who have simply disappeared. Sometimes a body is found, sometimes not. I have to go before they come." Instinctively I opened my arms to her and for a moment we held each other tightly. I knew my body felt as real to her as hers did to me, past and present colliding for just a few seconds of human contact.

And then there came a dreadful banging at the front door. A heavy fist shaking the wood so we felt, or imagined we did, the reverberations, or maybe that was just because we were both shaking. She pulled away. "It's too late, he's here. My soul mate, my secret lover, the father of my child. Now he wants me dead." I saw the resistance drain from her, saw her resign herself to the fact she had no choices. As she moved to go downstairs, I was powerless to intervene, a captive witness, I couldn't leave.

From where I stood, behind Hettie, I could see the five roughly-dressed men, smell the mix of soil, sweat and excitement coming off them. One stood taller above the others, thin and with self-confidence, the natural leader. He entered ahead of the others and as Hettie's gaze met his wolf eyes, shock ran through me like an electric bolt. Shoulder-length grey-streaked dark hair, pale skin, and those eyes. This then was Hettie's soul mate, this was Abe. He wasn't Seb, I could see that now, but the resemblance was too close for him to be anything other than a forebear. As I tried to assimilate what was happening, what I was witnessing, he was already manhandling her, ripping away her clothes and the last shreds of her dignity. The rest of the men crowded in, surrounding her now naked body.

And yet encircled and trapped as she was, shivering in the midst of the men and their fevered excitement, she drew herself up, stood tall and commanded his attention.

"You were my lover, father of my child, I loved you," she hissed, "Yet you do this, shame on you." In the noise and scuffle I almost missed the next words, dripping with venom, "Know that I have cursed you," she said. "You may kill me, but I will live on in that curse, and you will never, never forget me, throughout time."

And then she was gone, hidden from my sight by the men jostling around her, dragged away through the garden, pale skin caught and scratched by rough hands as well as by sharp stones when she stumbled, and twigs from the trees as they hauled her through the forest. They were taking her to the river. I had been here so often in my nightmares. I recognised the red, copper and yellow autumn colours, such beauty overseeing such ugliness. I rested my fingers briefly on my birthmark which I knew matched hers, and I was waiting on the banks of the river as they came towards me.

Her hair was matted, her body marked with scratches and deeper cuts, bruises already bloomed, but she'd turned her lovely face to the sinking sun. And when one of the men shook her to gain her attention, his "Don't struggle, woman," seemed superfluous. "We know what you are," he snarled, spittle hitting her face, "now it's proving time." Abe was silent; the eyes I knew so well, cold and unyielding. If he was regretting what he'd started, it didn't show. Did he truly believe Hettie was a witch or was this simply a convenient way of ridding himself of an unwanted lover? I wondered if he understood the strength of her curse, forged by betrayal and hate. If he didn't now, he would in the future.

Hettie was silent, she had the power to curse them all, but she chose not to. Her face still turned to the last rays of the sun as it lowered, she closed her eyes, and the men for a moment were silent too. It was time. I watched with fresh horror what I'd seen so often before, as they lowered her into the fast-flowing river, hands and feet bound. She didn't stand a chance.

CHAPTER 24

I came back with a start and opened my eyes to the present, with Seb leaning over me, wolf eyes identical to those I'd just watched oversee cold-blooded murder. My recoil was instinctive, my terror real. Hettie's words rang in my ears, and whilst I still didn't yet understand how or why, there was no doubt in my mind that Abe and Seb were interchangeable. Murder which ran in the blood of one, must run in the blood of the other.

I had to remain calm.

"You OK, what happened?" He tenderly stroked the hair back from my forehead. "You were out cold." I shivered, and he pulled the fleece throw from the back of the sofa and tucked it round me.

"I must have fainted, happens sometimes, low blood pressure." I pushed the fleece off me, saying, "I'm sorry, I think I'm going to be sick," and as I passed him there was no mistaking his expression of distaste.

I wasn't wrong, I was very sick indeed, then clinging to the sink for balance because I felt so woozy. I splashed cold water on my face, not stopping until my skin felt numb. The nausea had subsided; the memory of what I'd seen hadn't. I'd always been convinced Seb was my soul mate, that there was an unbreakable connection between us, but I'd never imagined our past could or would catch up with us the way it had.

As I came slowly back downstairs, Seb handed me a cold glass of water. He had his phone in the other hand. I knew he'd seen the message and was wondering whether I had. I drank and hauled myself as far back to normality as I could.

"I'm so sorry, sickness always follows the fainting. Sorry to spoil our last evening, but I think I just need to rest." I put a hand to my forehead and grimaced a little to indicate a headache.

"Right, I'll leave you to it." He shrugged, a look of relief on his face. "Not much use in a sickroom, I'm afraid." He smiled, but he wasn't kidding, there was no mistaking the aversion emanating from him.

I smiled back. "I'll be fine, just need an early night."

"If you need anything just give me a shout."

"Right," I said, and thought if I had to rely on him in a health emergency, I'd be in dead trouble.

"I'm away to London early in the morning, but I'll message you, let you know when I want to start moving my stuff in."

I wasn't sure I could keep my composure, but luckily he seemed as keen to go as I was to see the back of him.

"Will miss you," I said. He was busy checking his wallet and didn't answer. He gave me a cursory smile and grabbed his phone, and obviously a goodbye kiss wasn't on the agenda, maybe I'd repulsed him by throwing up. The moment the door clicked shut behind him, I ran for the security system panel. The cottage being fairly isolated, I'd spent a lot of money on a high tech system and never had I made a better decision. The shutters smoothly closed, and all the doors and windows automatically locked. I knew I was as safe as I could be. What my next move would be, was another question altogether.

I couldn't leave until I knew I had somewhere to stay, and anyway I wasn't in a fit state to drive. I needed to make a calm, measured plan. Looking around the room, which suddenly didn't feel as cosy as it should, I was sure he wouldn't be back tonight, but as an extra precaution I threw a protection spell around the cottage – touching Hettie's necklace protectively, which gave me an extra layer of confidence. Looking through the lens of my new knowledge, I was devastated. I saw how I'd been blinded by desire, had willingly let myself be manoeuvred into increasing isolation. I could have kicked myself, it was such an obvious tactic in an abusive relationship, I could be making a mistake in assuming Seb would act like Abe. But in my heart I knew beyond doubt, and violated as I felt, I was equally incensed. It was that cold anger I needed to hold on to, it would keep me alert and focused.

In that spirit I reviewed the message I'd seen; what was the meaning of the communication from Will? Was it possible Will, someone else I'd trusted, also meant me harm? What was the Purge? But I needed to put my distress and pondering on the back burner, swift action was what had to happen right now. I knew in my bones that grave danger was imminent, and another thought occurred; did he really intend to move in or was that when he'd strike? I was convinced I was destined for the same fate as Hettie, I'd drown in the river, I know he was fascinated by the site. I'd feared it since I'd moved in, and goodness knows I'd dreamt about it often enough. Seb had done his part in cutting me off from friends. It would be a good while before I'd be missed. I had to get away from Yorkshire, and I had to do it right away.

I decided I could only fit two large cases in the car, they'd have to do for the time being. The rest of my stuff could be packed and sent to a holding address, although such was my fear at this point, I'd decided I wasn't going to share my new address with anyone local. My heart was unbearably heavy, I knew I'd never come back to the moors, the beautiful, desolate place of my dreams had turned into a living nightmare. Having lovingly renovated Lavender Cottage, I knew I had to put it behind me, it was too dangerous to stay. I was convinced I had come under the eye of the dark side, those opposing the harmless magic of a White Witch, as to them there was no difference. A witch was a witch, and as such needed to be destroyed, all tarred with the same brush.

I sorted what I wanted to wear in the morning. Jeans, a warm jumper, slip-on comfortable loafers, woollen hat and a parka, all of which should cope well with the chill already in the air. Then I worked swiftly, sorting all my clothes into two piles, one for a new life, one that could wait and be sent on. When I'd dealt with the clothes, I set my hand to everything else. Taking out the *Book of Knowledge* gave me pause for thought. Should I leave it, hide it for the next inhabitant to find? How dangerous was possession? If I took it with me, would it tie me to danger? I shook my head; it meant too much to me to leave it. Wrapping it carefully in a couple of jumpers, I placed it at the bottom of one of the cases, and carried on filling both until all that was left was a pile of my exquisite Goth clothes. It hurt to abandon them but I had to change my look, disappear into the crowd. Inconspicuous was what I had to aim for, blending in was what I had to achieve. I still had the outfits Beth had dismissed as frumpy, they'd be my ticket to obscurity.

Stripping out of the beautiful sheer black dress I'd bought and put on for Seb, I felt repulsed, and ashamed of the woman I'd become over these last months. Having put on pyjamas that certainly didn't scream seduction, I wiped my face clean, removing deep red lipstick and dark kohled eyes. And then I needed to fall back on my magic, changing my raven black hair back to blonde highlighted. Once I'd done that, the woman looking back at me from the mirror was vastly different, pale and exhausted, but relieved.

I knew I had to get some sleep. I had a long journey ahead but first I booked a hotel halfway to London, an old country mansion converted to a luxury health spa, which looked very much off the beaten track. Having reserved and been assured they'd have a room ready whatever time

I wanted to check in, I gave into exhaustion and deep dreamless sleep until the shrill of the alarm woke me at 5.30am.

Having organised everything the night before, all I had to do in the chill of the morning was jump in the car – and leave my life. As I opened the blinds, it was starting to get light, but I still felt vulnerable as I disabled the security system. I didn't expect to see Seb looming outside, but even so when I looked out of the window, and there was no sign of life other than the dawn chorus, I breathed a small and perhaps unacknowledged sigh of relief. It was a clear dry morning, a good day for driving. I piled everything into the car as quickly as I could, despite myself glancing over my shoulder, then did a quick run round the cottage to check I hadn't left behind anything important. I'd thought this was the place I'd spend many years, if not a lifetime, my beloved, bewitched cottage, but locking the front door I didn't know that I'd ever be able to return.

I'd blocked Seb and Will on my phone, and switched my phone off; call me paranoid, but I couldn't run the risk of them tracking me in some way. All was quiet on the roads at this time, and I turned my mind away from the events of last night to focus on driving safely, breathing a sigh of relief when I crossed into a different county, leaving Yorkshire behind me. I'd never felt so fearful in my entire life. Another half hour and I pulled into a 24-hour fuel station. Even though common sense told me I was miles away, I still didn't want to call attention to myself, let alone be recognised. I pulled my hat down as low as I could and put my shades on; it was bright but cold and I was grateful for all my layers.

I thought I'd get snacks and drinks for the journey, and took a moment to register the headlines on the paper stand before I entered the shop. Then my heart stood still; they were all screaming the same story. I grabbed copies of the main papers, then a wire basket and rushed round shoving biscuits, drinks and fruit in as swiftly as I could. I took the opportunity for a few deep breaths in an aisle at the back of the shop. I felt sick and dizzy, didn't know whether I was hyperventilating. I had to pay for my purchases and get out of there. The woman behind the counter gave me a funny look.

"You alright, love?"

"Yeah, just in a bit of a rush." Could she go any slower? As she folded the papers she tutted, "Shocking, these problems in Whitby. Always said it'd come to no good, the types that come along for them festivals."

I didn't answer, didn't want conversation. I thanked her and hurried out, I desperately needed to get moving again.

A mile or so down the road, I found a suitable stopping place. It looked like the entrance to a local beauty spot, and this early there was no-one around. I glugged down nearly a whole bottle of water, ripped open some chocolate digestives, and that familiar taste, milk chocolate with a hint of salt, gave me the quick hit I needed as I tipped the newspapers from the bag.

"17th Century Witchcraft Laws Reinstated!"

The Prime Minister was quoted – 'This scourge of

society must be eliminated, even if we have to resort to practices we never dreamt we'd ever see again. We have taken the immediate decision to lock down Whitby, and the North Yorkshire Moors area. Every woman over the age of 18 in the surrounding area will be questioned, and properties searched. Similar restrictions will be rolled out in other areas should that be deemed necessary. Such practices are totally unacceptable in the 21st Century.'

I felt sick, wished I hadn't been so quick with the chocolate biscuits. I read on. It got worse. 'The Prime Minister has acknowledged and is grateful to Professor Seb Williams for chairing the inquiry into this crisis. Professor Williams and his team in various parts of the country have been working with the government. The professor will now be based in Edinburgh taking up his role as a government adviser, his expertise in the subject of Witches will guide our policies going forward.'

I shut my eyes for a moment's silent prayer to whoever was watching over me. I'd left only just in time, then with dread I realised I still had the *Book of Knowledge*. I hate to think what would have happened if Seb had found the book, or I had stayed a second longer at the cottage. I had to dispose of it, I could see no way I could keep it and there was no-one I could give it to without bringing danger to their door. As I set off again, turning the problem over and over, I passed a derelict cottage for sale. In another time and place it would have held great appeal, a doer-upper in a rural area and in its own grounds. I'd driven past before a thought occurred. Throwing the car into reverse, I parked outside the cottage, hurriedly unzipped and delved to the bottom of one of the cases, and extracted the precious book then wrapped it in several layers of newspaper.

Checking there was no-one around, I went into the back garden of the cottage. If someone did turn up, I could always say I'd seen the for sale sign and was interested. I tried the back door into the kitchen, and was surprised it opened easily. As I stepped into the kitchen, a mouse ran across my path, freaking me out, but there were no other signs of life. I stretched up and placed the parcel on the top shelf of one of the kitchen cupboards. Nothing could link the book back to me. I knew it would be safer to destroy it, but couldn't bear to do that. Hopefully when things had died down, some other recipient would put it to good use – the legacy of the knowledge passed to another generation. I no longer needed it, I knew what I was doing now, I didn't need a book anymore. But as I made to leave, Hettie's words came back to me. I was the custodian of the knowledge, I could not simply abandon it. I retrieved it from the shelf, thinking hard; one of my friends worked in Hatton Garden, maybe I could package and courier it to be placed in a security box. Reversing my actions, I unwrapped the newspaper coverings and secured it again, safe in one of my jumpers in my suitcase. I had to find a solution that wouldn't leave me guilt-stricken at wiping out history.

A couple more hours brought me to the hotel. It looked lush, very much my sort of place and perfect to take my mind off what I was running from, and the decadent black and white marble floor and luxurious décor in reception only confirmed this. On impulse when the man behind the desk welcomed me to Mill House, I asked if by chance they had availability if I wanted to stay a few days more. They did, and instead of a few extra days I found myself booking a full two weeks. The icing on the cake was that they upgraded me from a standard double to the honeymoon suite at no extra cost. I felt there was an element of irony in that, in light of my recent romantic entanglement. Looking around I took a deep breath. I owed it to myself to take time to de-stress, and first thing on the list was a swim. As I changed into my swimsuit I put my phone on to charge. There was a message from a number I didn't recognise. Hoping it wasn't Seb using someone else's phone, I cautiously opened it, but it wasn't Seb, it was Luke, and he sounded desperate.

> Ellie, please call! Lottie's disappeared, thought she might be with you at the cottage, but you're not there either. Anna's not answering her phone, what's going on? Are you OK? Please, please call ASAP! Luke.

I broke out in a cold sweat; a shiver ran down my spine, had the Purge started already? I'd left, but had I gone far enough? Was I safe? I was distraught that Lottie had gone missing, my instinct told me it was unlikely she'd turn up – alive that is, and where was Anna? How on earth had we, Lottie and I and the rest of the Mystical Ladies imagined we could keep our magic under wraps? Thinking back, even one of the guys at Alice's wedding had heard rumours about Whitby. But could I trust Luke? Maybe he was in on it. Spiralling fear governed my next move. With trembling fingers I deleted the message and blocked his number. Then I deleted all my Yorkshire contacts, including the Mystical Ladies. I deleted the WhatsApp group, removed the SIM card, snapped it in half – just in case – and flushed it down the toilet. As a final act, I wrapped my phone in newspaper, laid it on the floor and smashed it to smithereens with one of my heavy boots, hitting it with all the pent up emotion I was feeling. I had to stay safe, and under the radar, I no longer knew who was a friend and who a foe.

I'd order a new phone tomorrow, a new number, a new start far away from Whitby, the North Yorkshire Moors, and the darkness I'd found there. That was the only sensible course of action. I took the spell book out again to rewrap and conceal it more securely in the lining of my case; it was like an old familiar friend now, I felt protective. Although going forward I'd have no further use for it, useless spells for a modern-day woman, weren't they? After all, I wasn't going to dabble in magic again. Stay away from trouble, that was my new mantra. I'd keep it just in case though until I could decide what to do with it – my only link to Hettie and the past, but that was all it would be, simply a memory. No harm in that, was there?

LETTER TO MY READERS

Thank you for choosing to read my debut novel, part one of Ellie's story. I hope you enjoyed reading it as much as I enjoyed writing about this sassy woman. I started Ellie's story in late 2019, never imagining that I would have so much time on my hands to write following our first Covid lockdown in March 2020. Writing kept my mind occupied, and maybe I went to darker places because of what was happening around us.

I loved writing Ellie's story so much that I couldn't stop with book one, *Dream Die Repeat*. If you want to know what happens next, please look out for *Not Forever Dead* in early 2023.

I took a leap of faith, after 38 years working in the world of finance, and registered for a creative writing course with the Open University in early 2019. Through interaction with other writers online, I had some pretty encouraging comments. One of the projects was to write a short story about a lady on a bus, wearing a red jumper and carrying a Pekinese on her knee, also wearing a red jumper. I decided that she was a Witch who had cast a spell on her best friend, turning her into a dog. Something had gone wrong with the spell, and she was unable to change her back. So she was on the bus, heading to the next town to visit a wise woman who could help. The readers loved it, and the idea of Ellie was conceived.

The inspiration for Lavender Cottage – based in a fictitious village – is our very own North Yorkshire Moors 18th Century cottage, originally built in 1755. My husband Tom inherited Fern cottage in the delightful village of Lealholm – just 9 miles from the historic town of Whitby – nestled in the North Yorkshire Moors National Park. We spent nearly 3 years lovingly renovating Fern Cottage, and we did actually find the storeroom full to the brim with some interesting stuff, just like Ellie did. Stripping the modern wallpaper, we decided to expose the original Yorkshire stone, and we found different layers of life, from 1980s wallpaper, to tiny rose bud paper from Victorian times, and Georgian green paint. We also found initials carved into the stone above our open fireplace in the kitchen, and just outside the kitchen door. It made me wonder, who lived here over the centuries since its first residents. If you would like to see the cottage for yourself, it is now available as a holiday let through www.Cottages.com (reference UK30911) We have 10/10 for reviews, our guests love the cottage. You can also email me for more information: julie.langton@hotmail.co.uk.

We have been visiting the North Yorkshire Moors and the historic seaside town of Whitby, since the early 1980's, a magical place with the Dracula connection and the bi-annual Goth Festivals, amongst other wonderful festivals in this area. Like Ellie we also have 2 holiday let properties at Whitehall Landing, as we love Whitby so much. We let these out through www.cottages.com (ref UK2654 and UK32644), we hope you enjoy the area as much as we do, and of course Ellie fell in love with the place!

I must mention my love for music, and especially Kate Bush! I remember seeing 'Wuthering Heights' on *Top of the Pops* as a teenager, and from that moment on I was captivated. I started writing this book in late 2019, and finished it towards the end of 2020. As you can imagine I am elated that Kate Bush has had a resurgence further to 'Stranger Things', and I hope that I can introduce you to other Kate Bush tracks that you may not have heard.

My own music tastes are a little different from Ellie's – I am more of a rock chick. I love Led Zeppelin, Pink Floyd and Genesis, The Beatles, Radiohead, the Artic Monkeys, and Muse to name a few! I do also really love what I call "chill out music" bands such as Air and Zero 7. Ellie however has her own mind, she is obsessed with 80s alternative music, some of the bands she has listened to are Japan, The Cure, and Siouxsie and the Banshees, she didn't really appreciate my music tastes!

As I was doing my research, I came across a British band called Broadcast. Although they don't feature in this book, when I wanted some spooky inspiration, I listened to their music. I can imagine if this book ever becomes a series or a film, their music would be the perfect sound track, especially the spooky 'The Book Lovers'. Sadly, their vocalist Trish Keenan died on 14th January 2011, but her music lives on.

ACKNOWLEDGEMENTS

A massive thank you to Tom, my very own soulmate, what a fabulous journey this has been. You believed in me right from the start and have followed Ellie's journey since the first seed of an idea in 2019. You have patiently listened and contributed, taking Ellie to some dark places. You say it straight and I have really appreciated your constructive criticism. I have tried not to bore you, reading paragraphs to you, night after night, and you have taken it all patiently in your stride.

A huge thank you to my early readers, Sally Gregory, Scot Imrie-Kuzu, Lesley Love, Zoe Pinnock, Kate Ramsey and Karen Serdeczna. Some of you have read the manuscript in its rawest form, well before editing. I appreciate every one of you taking time out to read my work and for your honest feedback. Thank you, David Hannah for coming up with the title, *Dream Die Repeat*, I love it. Thank you to the Roe's – Kathy and Malcolm for coming up with some magical ideas.

To my amazing editor Marilyn Messik, we have worked so well together. So well that Book two in the trilogy, *Not Forever Dead*, is nearly ready to be sent to the Publisher. This is my first experience of editing and Marilyn has patiently explained why some paragraphs, sentences and conversations have ended up on the cutting room floor, even though it seemed brutal at the time!

I met Sarah my wonderful publisher at Goldcrest Books through business networking when I was a financial adviser. Never in a million years did I think I would submit a finished novel to be published. Sarah has been brilliant at explaining the publishing journey, and introduced me to my editor, who has herself written some spooky books. She thought we'd be the perfect fit. It's been amazing to work with you on this book, and there will be more to come.

Last, but not least, I have to thank my primary school teacher Tom Wilson for inspiring me to write and reach my full potential. From the age of 9 to 11, you pushed the boundaries of my reading experience with books such as *Lord of the Flies*, Ray Bradbury science fiction, and my all-time favourite book, *Cider with Rosie*. I loved your class and I learnt so much in those two years, a 1970s carefree childhood was just the best. Sorry it's taken so long but here is my homework, you always said I had tenacity. I think my 9-year-old self, would be particularly impressed, don't you?